A STUDY ON THE BOOK OF ROMANS

By: Dr. Christopher Bowen

CSB Ministires
5880 Old Dixie Road, Forest Park, GA 30297
E-mail: drcbowen@aol.com

Unless otherwise indicated, all Scripture quotations are taken from the Holy Bible, New International Version.

Copyright © 2006 by Dr. Christopher Bowen
All rights reserved
No portion of this work may be reproduced, stored in a retrieval system, or transmitted in any form or by any means electronic, mechanical photocopy, recording, or any other except for brief quotations in printed reviews, without the prior permission of the Publisher.

Printing by: Lulu Press

USA ISBN   978-0-6151-3490-1

Table of Contents

Introduction 7

Romans 1 13

Romans 2 22

Romans 3 30

Romans 4 39

Romans 5 47

Romans 6 56

Romans 7 64

Romans 8 72

Romans 9 82

Romans 10 92

Romans 11 100

Romans 12 109

Romans 13 116

Romans 14 123

Romans 15 131

Romans 16 140

Answer Guide 149

Introduction

AUTHOR: PAUL, the apostle (**1:1**)

PLACE OF WRITING: CORINTH; as evident from the greetings of Gaius, who lived at Corinth (**16:23; 1 Co 1:14**), and the Erastus, who had settled down there (**16:23; 2 Ti 4:20**). Also, Phoebe, who apparently accompanied the epistle (**16:1-2**), was from the church at Cenchrea, a "suburb" of Corinth.

TIME OF WRITING: 57-58 A.D.; while on his third journey (**Ac 20:1-3**), just prior to his arrival to Jerusalem with the collection for the needy saints (**15:25-26; Ac 20:16; 24:17**).

BACKGROUND OF THE CHURCH AT ROME: Nothing is revealed in the New Testament as to the start of the church in Rome. It is possible that visitors to

Jerusalem on the day of Pentecost following the Lord's ascension were among the 3000 saved and later took the gospel with them back home (**Ac 2:10**). Or it could be that among those dispersed following Stephen's death were some that went to Rome and preached the gospel there (**Ac 8:1-4**).

The first we read of Christians from Rome is possibly that of Aquila and Pricilla, who along with all Jews were expelled from Rome by Claudius and were found by Paul at Corinth during his second journey (**Ac 18:1-2**). After traveling with Paul to Ephesus and working with the church there (**Ac 18:18-19, 24-26; 1 Co 16:19**), we find them back at Rome and hosting a church in their house (**16:3-5**).

From the greetings given by Paul in chapter sixteen, it appears that there were several churches in Rome meeting in various homes (**16:5, 14, 15**). The names of individuals would suggest that the Christians were primarily Gentiles, with a smaller number of Jews.

The reputation of the Christians in Rome was widespread; both their faith (**1:8**) and obedience (**16:19**) were well known. For this reason Paul had long wanted to see them (**15:23**), with the goal of sharing in their mutual edification (**1:11-12**) and to be assisted on his way to Spain (**15:22-24**).

PURPOSE OF WRITING: Paul expresses in this epistle that he had for some time planned to preach the gospel at Rome (**1:13-15**) and from there go on to Spain (**15:22-24**). Though he still had these intentions (**15:28-29**), the spreading cancer of the "Judaizing teachers" which had disrupted churches in Antioch, Corinth and Galatia was likely to make its way to Rome. To prevent this, and to assure that his visit to Rome would be a pleasant one (**15:30-33**), Paul writes:

TO SET STRAIGHT THE DESIGN AND NATURE OF THE GOSPEL

In doing so, he demonstrates how the gospel of Christ fulfills what is lacking in both heathenism and Judaism, thereby effectively replacing them as religious systems. Such an epistle would arm the church at Rome against those who would pervert the gospel or suggest that it was inadequate by itself.

THEME: Romans 1:16-17

> **"For I am not ashamed of the gospel of Christ, for it is the power of God to salvation for everyone who believes, for the Jew first and also for the Greek. For in it the righteousness of God is revealed from faith to faith; as it is written, 'The just shall live by faith.'"**

In these two verses Paul states his confidence in the gospel and the reasons for it. The bulk of his epistle is devoted to explaining why and how the gospel of Christ is God's power to save those who believe.

BRIEF OUTLINE

INTRODUCTION (1:1-17)

    I. <u>**JUSTIFICATION BY FAITH**</u> **(1:18-11:36)**

        A. SIN – THE "NEED" FOR SALVATION
1. The Need of the Gentiles (**1:18-2:16**)
2. The Need of the Jews (**2:17-3:8**)
3. The Universal Need for Salvation (**3:9-20**)

        B. JUSTIFICATION BY FAITH – THE "PROVISION" MADE FOR SALVATION
1. God's Righteousness Through Faith (**3:21-31**)
2. Abraham As An Example (**4:1-25**)

        C. FREEDOM – THE "RESULT" OF SALVATION
1. Freedom From Wrath (**5:1-21**)
2. Freedom From Sin (**6:1-23**)
3. Freedom From the Law (**7:1-25**)
4. Freedom From Death (**8:1-39**)

D. JEW AND GENTILE – THE "SCOPE" OF SALVATION
   1. God Chooses to Save Believers (**9:1-33**)
   2. Israel Chose to Trust in Their Own Righteousness (**10:1-21**)
   3. Both Jew and Gentile Can Have Salvation Through Faith (**11:1-36**)

II. **THE TRANSFORMED LIFE** (12:1-15:13)

   A. IN RELATION TO OVERALL CONDUCT (12:1-21)

   B. IN RELATION TO CIVIL AUTHORITY (13:1-7)

   C. IN RELATION TO FELLOW MAN (13:8-14)

   D. IN RELATION TO WEAK BRETHREN (14:1-15:13)

III. CONCLUDING REMARKS, INSTRUCTIONS, AND BENEDICTION (15:14-16:27)

REVIEW QUESTIONS FOR INTRODUCTION

1) Who wrote the epistle to the Romans?

_____

_____

2) From where was it written?

_____

_____

3) What is the approximate date of writing?

_____

_____

4) What is the purpose of this epistle?

_____

_____

5) Where is the theme of this epistle stated?

_____

_____

Chapter One

OBJECTIVES IN STUDYING THIS CHAPTER

1) To be impressed with the all-sufficiency of the gospel

2) To see how God's wrath may be directed toward our society today

OUTLINE

I. <u>INTRODUCTION & THEME</u> (1-17)

    A. CONCERNING PAUL (1-5)
1. His place in life: servant & apostle (**1**)
2. His story in life: the gospel of Christ (**2-4**)

3. His purpose in life: to produce obedience based on faith (**5**)

B. CONCERNING THE ROMANS (6-15)
1. Paul's description of them (**6-7**)
2. Paul's report of them (**8**)
3. Paul's deep desire to visit them (**9-10**)
4. Paul's reason and eagerness to visit them (**11-15**)

C. CONCERNING THE GOSPEL (16-17)
1. Its respectability: nothing to be ashamed of (**16a**)
2. Its nature: the power of God (**16b**)
3. Its aim: salvation (**16c**)
4. Its scope: for everyone who believes (**16d**)
5. Its content: the revelation of God's righteousness through faith (**17**)

II. <u>THE GENTILES' NEED OF SALVATION</u> (18-32)

A. WICKED MAN DISHONORING GOD (18-23)
1. Wicked man stifling God's revealed truth (**18-19**)
2. Wicked man despising the testimony of nature (**20**)
3. Wicked man ungrateful and foolish (**21-22**)

4. Wicked man given to idolatry (**23**)

  B. **HOLY GOD "GIVING UP" ON WICKED MAN (24-32)**
     1. Giving them up to disgusting uncleanness (**24-25**)
     2. Giving them up to lesbianism and homosexuality (**26-27**)
     3. Giving them up to debased minds and all unrighteousness (**28-32**)

SUMMARY

As is the custom in most of his epistles, Paul begins by extending greetings and offering thanks. Identifying himself as a bond-servant of Christ, he mentions his apostleship and its mission in the gospel of God concerning His Son: to bring about the obedience of faith among all the Gentiles.

> *Romans 1:1-6 (NIV) ¹Paul, a servant of Christ Jesus, called to be an apostle and set apart for the gospel of God— ²the gospel he promised beforehand through his prophets in the Holy Scriptures ³regarding his Son, who as to his human nature was a descendant of David, ⁴and who through the Spirit of holiness was declared with power to be the Son of God by his resurrection from the dead: Jesus Christ our Lord. ⁵Through him and for his name's sake, we received grace and apostleship to call people from among all the Gentiles to the obedience that comes*

from faith. ⁶And you also are among those who are called to belong to Jesus Christ.

Addressing the recipients of his epistle as "all who are beloved in Rome, called as saints," he extends to them the popular two-fold greeting of that day: "grace" and "peace."

Romans 1:7 (NIV)   *To all in Rome who are loved by God and called to be saints: Grace and peace to you from God our Father and from the Lord Jesus Christ.*

He is thankful for their well-known faith and reveals his desire to visit Rome and to proclaim the gospel there.

Romans 1:8-13 (NIV)   *⁸First, I thank my God through Jesus Christ for all of you, because your faith is being reported all over the world. ⁹God, whom I serve with my whole heart in preaching the gospel of his Son, is my witness how constantly I remember you ¹⁰in my prayers at all times; and I pray that now at last by God's will the way may be opened for me to come to you. ¹¹I long to see you so that I may impart to you some spiritual gift to make you strong— ¹²that is, that you and I may be mutually encouraged by each other's faith. ¹³I do not want you to be unaware, brothers, that I planned many times to come to you (but have been prevented from doing so until now) in order*

> *that I might have a harvest among you, just as I have had among the other Gentiles.*

The motivation behind that desire is his sense of obligation and bold conviction that the gospel is God's power to save.

> ***Romans 1:14-17 (NIV)** ¹⁴I am obligated both to Greeks and non-Greeks, both to the wise and the foolish. ¹⁵That is why I am so eager to preach the gospel also to you who are at Rome. ¹⁶I am not ashamed of the gospel, because it is the power of God for the salvation of everyone who believes: first for the Jew, then for the Gentile. ¹⁷For in the gospel a righteousness from God is revealed, a righteousness that is by faith from first to last, just as it is written: "The righteous will live by faith."*

The mention of "salvation" naturally leads to the need for all men to be saved. Paul begins to demonstrate this need on the part of the Gentiles. He explains that because of the Gentiles' failure to acknowledge the external power and divine nature of God as revealed in the world around them, and for their subsequent pride and idolatry, they were therefore exposed to God's wrath from heaven.

> ***Romans 1:18-23 (NIV)** ¹⁸The wrath of God is being revealed from heaven against all the*

godlessness and wickedness of men who suppress the truth by their wickedness, [19]since what may be known about God is plain to them, because God has made it plain to them. [20]For since the creation of the world God's invisible qualities—his eternal power and divine nature—have been clearly seen, being understood from what has been made, so that men are without excuse. [21]For although they knew God, they neither glorified him as God nor gave thanks to him, but their thinking became futile and their foolish hearts were darkened. [22]Although they claimed to be wise, they became fools [23]and exchanged the glory of the immortal God for images made to look like mortal man and birds and animals and reptiles.

This wrath manifested itself in God simply letting them reap the fruits of the vanity. By giving them over "to uncleanness, in the lusts of their hearts," "to vile passions," and "to a debased mind," the result was such corruption that even those who knew better were caught in its clutches.

Romans 1:24-32 (NIV)   *[24]Therefore God gave them over in the sinful desires of their hearts to sexual impurity for the degrading of their bodies with one another. [25]They exchanged the truth of God for a lie, and worshiped and served created things rather than the Creator—who is forever praised. Amen. [26]Because of this, God gave them over to shameful lusts. Even their women exchanged natural relations for unnatural ones. [27]In the same way the men also abandoned natural relations with women and were inflamed with lust for one another. Men committed indecent acts with other men, and received in themselves the due penalty for their perversion. [28]Furthermore, since they did not think it worthwhile to retain the knowledge of God, he gave them over to a depraved mind, to do what ought not to be done. [29]They have become filled with every kind of wickedness, evil, greed and depravity. They are full of envy, murder, strife, deceit and malice. They are gossips, [30]slanderers, God-haters, insolent, arrogant and boastful; they invent ways of doing evil; they disobey their parents; [31]they are senseless, faithless, heartless, ruthless. [32]Although they know God's righteous decree that those who do such things deserve death, they not only continue to do these very things but also approve of those who practice them.*

REVIEW QUESTIONS FOR THE CHAPTER

1) List the two main points of this chapter

_____

_____

2) How was Jesus declared to be the Son of God? **(4)**

_____

_____

3) What was the objective of Paul's apostleship? **(5)**

_____

_____

4) Why did Paul want to go to Rome? **(11-12)**

_____

_____

5) To whom was Paul obligated? **(14)**

_____

_____

6) What is God's power to save? (**16**)

_____

_____

7) Why is it God's power to save? (**17**)

_____

_____

8) What tow invisible attributes of God are revealed in nature? (**20**)

_____

_____

9) How does God express His wrath? (**24, 26, 28**)

_____

_____

10) What one sin in particular is an indication that God's wrath toward man is in full force? (**26, 27**)

_____

_____

Chapter Two

OBJECTIVES IN STUDYING THIS CHAPTER

1) To see how people without a direct revelation of God's will can still be lost.
2) To see how people who may have a written law from God are also in need of salvation.

OUTLINE

I. <u>**THE GENTILES' NEED OF SALVATION**</u> **(1-16)**

A. **EVEN THE "JUDGES" WILL BE JUDGED (1-11)**
1. The inconsistent judge judges himself **(1)**
2. The hypocritical judge is judged by truth **(2)**
3. The foolish judge reasons poorly **(3)**

4. The presumptuous judge treasures up wrath (**4-11**)

B. NOT HAVING A "WRITTEN" LAW DOES NOT EXEMPT FROM JUDGMENT (12-16)
   1. Those who sin will still perish (**12**)
   2. The Gentiles DO have the law (**13-15**)
   3. Jesus Christ will judge accordingly (**16**)

II. THE JEWS' NEED OF SALVATION (17-29)

A. THE JEWS CONDEMNED BY THEIR OWN LAW (17-24)
   1. The Jewish self-portrait (**17-20**)
   2. The Jewish inconsistency and dishonor of God (**21-24**)

B. THE LIMITATION OF CIRCUMCISION (25-29)
   1. Voided by transgressing the Law (**25-27**)
   2. The true Jew is one circumcised in the heart, in the Spirit (**28-29**)

SUMMARY

Having vividly depicted the condition of the Gentile world in chapter one, Paul now addresses his comments to those who pass judgment on others when they themselves are guilty of the same things.

> *Romans 2:1 (NIV) You, therefore, have no excuse, you who pass judgment on someone else, for at whatever point you judge the other, you are condemning yourself, because you who pass judgment do the same things.*

He points out that they are in danger of God's righteous judgment, who "will render to each one according to his deeds."

> *Romans 2:2-6 (NIV) ²Now we know that God's judgment against those who do such things is based on truth. ³So when you, a mere man, pass judgment on them and yet do the same things, do you think you will escape God's judgment? ⁴Or do you show contempt for the riches of his kindness, tolerance and patience, not realizing that God's kindness leads you toward repentance? ⁵But because of your stubbornness and your unrepentant heart, you are storing up wrath against yourself for the day of God's wrath, when his righteous judgment will be revealed. ⁶God "will give to each person according to what he has done."*

This judgment will offer either eternal life or wrath and indignation, given without partiality, and the decision is based on whether one does good or evil.

> *Romans 2:7-11 (NIV) ⁷To those who by persistence in doing good seek glory, honor and immortality, he will give eternal life. ⁸But for those who are self-seeking and who reject the truth and follow evil, there will be wrath and anger. ⁹There will be trouble and distress for every human being who does evil: first for the Jew, then for the Gentile; ¹⁰but glory, honor and peace for everyone who does good: first for the Jew, then for the Gentile. ¹¹For God does not show favoritism.*

To justify the condemnation of Gentiles who did not have a written law (like the Jews), Paul affirms that the Gentiles could "by nature do the things contained in the law" and that their own consciences will bear witness of their guilt on the day of judgment. In this way Paul demonstrated the Gentiles' need of salvation.

> *Romans 2:12-16 (NIV) ¹²All who sin apart from the law will also perish apart from the law, and all who sin under the law will be judged by the law. ¹³For it is not those who hear the law who are righteous in God's sight, but it is those who obey the law who will be declared righteous. ¹⁴(Indeed, when Gentiles, who do not have the law, do by nature things required by the law, they are a law for themselves, even though they do not have the law, ¹⁵since they show that the requirements of the law are written on their hearts, their consciences also bearing witness, and their thoughts now accusing,*

now even defending them.) ¹⁶This will take place on the day when God will judge men's secrets through Jesus Christ, as my gospel declares.

Lest the Jews think their having the law frees them from condemnation, Paul proceeds to demonstrate that they too are in need of salvation. Though they have the law, their failure to keep it perfectly caused them to dishonor God and blaspheme His name.

Romans 1:17-24 (NIV) ¹⁷Now you, if you call yourself a Jew; if you rely on the law and brag about your relationship to God; ¹⁸if you know his will and approve of what is superior because you are instructed by the law; ¹⁹if you are convinced that you are a guide for the blind, a light for those who are in the dark, ²⁰an instructor of the foolish, a teacher of infants, because you have in the law the embodiment of knowledge and truth— ²¹you, then, who teach others, do you not teach yourself? You who preach against stealing, do you steal? ²²You who say that people should not commit adultery, do you commit adultery? You who abhor idols, do you rob temples? ²³You who brag about the law, do you dishonor God by breaking the law? ²⁴As it is written: "God's name is blasphemed among the Gentiles because of you."

Introducing a thought he will expand upon later in the epistle, he points out that a true Jew is one who is circumcised in his heart, and not just in the flesh.

> *Romans 2:25-29 (NIV)* *25Circumcision has value if you observe the law, but if you break the law, you have become as though you had not been circumcised. 26If those who are not circumcised keep the law's requirements, will they not be regarded as though they were circumcised? 27The one who is not circumcised physically and yet obeys the law will condemn you who, even though you have the written code and circumcision, are a lawbreaker. 28A man is not a Jew if he is only one outwardly, nor is circumcision merely outward and physical. 29No, a man is a Jew if he is one inwardly; and circumcision is circumcision of the heart, by the Spirit, not by the written code. Such a man's praise is not from men, but from God.*

REVIEW QUESTIONS FOR THE CHAPTER

1) List the main points of this chapter

_____

_____

2) Why is one who passes judgment without excuse?

_____

_____

3) How does God try to lead one to repentance? **(4)**

_____

_____

4) What is the reward given to those who do good? To those who do evil? **(9,10)**

_____

_____

5) How will God judge those who do not have a "written" law? **(14-16)**

_____

_____

6) Without a "written" Law, how did the Gentiles know the difference between right and wrong? (**14,15**)

_____

_____

7) Why were the Jews in need of salvation? (**21-24**)

_____

_____

Chapter Three

OBJECTIVES IN STUDYING THIS CHAPTER

1) To understand the particulars of God's righteousness: grace, redemption, propitiations, faith in Jesus, and justification.
2) To see the difference between a law of works and the law of faith.

OUTLINE

  I. <u>THE JEWS' NEED OF SALVATION</u> (1-20)

    A. THE JEWISH ADVANTAGE (1-2)
      1. In many respects (**1**)
      2. Especially in having the "Oracles of God" (**2**)

    B. ANSWERS TO POSSIBLE OBJECTIONS (3-8)

1. Unbelieving Jews will not make the faithfulness of God without effect (**3-4**)
2. God is right to be angry, even if "unrighteousness" demonstrates His own righteousness (**5-6**)
3. Though sin might increase God's truth and give Him glory, people will still be judged for their sins (**7-8**)

C. **THE JEWS INDICTED AS SINNERS BY THEIR OWN SCRIPTURES (9-20)**
   1. Despite advantages, Jews like Greeks are under sin (**9**)
   2. Biblical proof (**10-18**)
   3. Application and conclusion (**19-20**)
   4. The Law condemns all, especially to whom it was given (**19**)
   5. Law cannot justify, but only reveal the knowledge of sin (**20**)

II. **THE PROVISION: JUSTIFICATION BY FAITH (21-31)**

A. **GOD'S RIGHTEOUSNESS REVEALED (21-23)**
   1. Apart from law, but witnessed by the Law (**21**)
   2. A righteousness through faith in Jesus (**22a**)
   3. For all who believe, for all have sinned (**22b-23**)

B. **GOD'S RIGHTEOUSNESS EXPLAINED (24-26)**

1. Justification by grace through redemption in Christ (**24**)
2. Jesus' blood offered by God as a propitiation through faith (**25a**)
3. This demonstrates God's righteousness toward the one who has faith in Jesus (**25b-26**)

C. IMPLICATIONS OF GOD'S RIGHTEOUSNESS (27-31)
1. Boasting on man's part is excluded (**27a**)
2. For justification is based on faith, not deeds of law (**27b-28**)
3. God is God of Jews and Gentiles, for he justifies both by faith (**29-30**)
4. This does not void the need for law, but rather meets the requirements of law (**31**)

SUMMARY

As Paul continues to demonstrate the Jews' need of salvation, he proceeds to answer questions that he envisions protesting Jews might ask. He explains the advantage of being a Jew, the faithfulness of God in spite of the Jews' unbelief, and the right of God to condemn the unrighteousness of man even though it magnifies His own righteousness.

Romans 3:1-8 (NIV) ¹*What advantage, then, is there in being a Jew, or what value is there in circumcision?* ²*Much in every way!*

First of all, they have been entrusted with the very words of God. ³What if some did not have faith? Will their lack of faith nullify God's faithfulness? ⁴Not at all! Let God be true, and every man a liar. As it is written:

"So that you may be proved right when you speak and prevail when you judge." ⁵But if our unrighteousness brings out God's righteousness more clearly, what shall we say? That God is unjust in bringing his wrath on us? (I am using a human argument.) ⁶Certainly not! If that were so, how could God judge the world? ⁷Someone might argue, "If my falsehood enhances God's truthfulness and so increases his glory, why am I still condemned as a sinner?" ⁸Why not say—as we are being slanderously reported as saying and as some claim that we say—"Let us do evil that good may result"? Their condemnation is deserved.

Though the Jews had the advantage of possessing the oracles of God, Paul still concludes that the Jews as well as the Gentiles are in sin and proves his conclusion by listing a series of Old Testament scriptures that speaks to those under the law (the Jews) as sinners.

Romans 3:9-19 (NIV) ⁹What shall we conclude then? Are we any better? Not at all! We have already made the charge that Jews and Gentiles alike are all under sin. ¹⁰As it is written: "There is no one righteous, not even one; ¹¹there is no one who understands, no one who seeks God. ⁱ²All have turned away, they have together become worthless; there is no one who does good, not even one." ¹³"Their throats are open graves; their tongues practice deceit." "The poison of vipers is on their lips." ¹⁴"Their mouths are full of cursing and bitterness." ¹⁵"Their feet are swift to shed blood; ¹⁶ruin and misery mark their ways, ¹⁷and the way of peace they do not know." ¹⁸"There is no fear of God before their eyes." ¹⁹Now we know that whatever the law says, it says to those who are under the law, so that every mouth may be silenced and the whole world held accountable to God.

His conclusion: a law (like the Law of Moses) could not save, but only reveal the knowledge of sin; a point he will elaborate upon in chapter seven.

Romans 3:20 (NIV) *Therefore no one will be declared righteous in his sight by observing the law; rather, through the law we become conscious of sin.*

Paul now carefully begins to explain the "good news" of God's plan of salvation. Apart from law, yet witnessed by the Law and the Prophets, God's way of making man right through faith in Jesus Christ is now made clear, and made available to all who believe, whether Jew or Greek, for all have sinned.

> *Romans 3:21-23 (NIV) ²¹But now a righteousness from God, apart from law, has been made known, to which the Law and the Prophets testify. ²²This righteousness from God comes through faith in Jesus Christ to all who believe. There is no difference, ²³for all have sinned and fall short of the glory of God,*

This justification of man is explained in terms of redemption, made possible through the blood of Christ, and offered to those who have faith in Christ. It also demonstrates how God can be both "just" (who takes seriously the sins of mankind) and " a justifier" (who is able to forgive sinners). God is able to do this by offering Christ's blood as a propitiation to those who have faith

> *Romans 3:24-26 (NIV) ²⁴and are justified freely by his grace through the redemption that came by Christ Jesus. ²⁵God presented him as a sacrifice of atonement, through faith in his blood. He did this to demonstrate his justice, because in his forbearance he had left the sins committed beforehand unpunished— ²⁶he did it to demonstrate his justice at the present time, so as to be just and the one who justifies those who have faith in Jesus.*

This "justification" is a gift of God's grace to those who have faith, which prevents anyone from boasting as though they through the works of a law deserved it.

> **Romans 3:27-30 (NIV)** [27]**Where, then, is boasting? It is excluded. On what principle? On that of observing the law? No, but on that of faith.** [28]**For we maintain that a man is justified by faith apart from observing the law.** [29]**Is God the God of Jews only? Is he not the God of Gentiles too? Yes, of Gentiles too,** [30]**since there is only one God, who will justify the circumcised by faith and the uncircumcised through that same faith.**

This does not void the need for law, but rather meets the requirement of law.

> **Romans 3:31 (NIV) Do we, then, nullify the law by this faith? Not at all! Rather, we uphold the law.**

REVIEW QUESTIONS FOR THE CHAPTER

1) List the main points of this chapter

_____

_____

2) What advantage was there in being a Jew? **(2)**

_____

_____

3) What comes through law? **(20)**

_____

_____

4) What came apart from law? **(21)**

_____

_____

5) Who has sinned? **(23)**

_____

_____

6) What is the gift of God's grace? (**24**)

_____

_____

7) How is God appeased for our sins? (**25**)

_____

_____

8) How does man receive justification from God? (**28**)

_____

_____

9) How does "justification by faith" relate to the principle of law? (**31**)

_____

_____

Chapter Four

OBJECTIVES IN STUDYING THIS CHAPTER

1) To understand how Abraham was justified in God's sight
2) To see that the "righteousness" God imputes to man is actually justification (i.e., forgiveness)
3) To comprehend the nature of justifying faith by considering the example of Abraham

OUTLINE

I. <u>JUSTIFICATION OF ABRAHAM AS AN EXAMPLE</u> (1-8)

   A. HOW ABRAHAM WAS JUSTIFIED (1-5)
      1. If by works, then he could boast (**1-2**)
      2. The Scriptures reveal it was by his faith in God (**3**)
      3. One who trusts in works, seeks God's debt, not His grace (**4**)

4. But when one trusts in God to justify him, such faith is counted for righteousness (**5**)

B. THE TESTIMONY OF DAVID (6-8)
1. Even David spoke of God imputing righteousness apart from works (**6**)
2. Blessed are those against whom God does not impute sins (**7-8**)

II. <u>RIGHTEOUSNESS BY FAITH AVAILABLE TO ALL BELIEVERS</u> (9-25)

A. BECAUSE ABRAHAM WAS JUSTIFIED BEFORE CIRCUMCISION (9-12)
1. His faith was counted for righteousness before he was circumcised (**9-10**)
2. Circumcised was a seal of the righteousness he had while uncircumcised (**11a**)
3. Thus he became the father of all who have the same kind of faith, both circumcised and uncircumcised (**11b-12**)

B. BECAUSE THE PROMISE TO ABRAHAM WAS GRANTED THROUGH FAITH (13-25)
1. The promise to be the heir of the world given in view of his faith (**13**)
2. It was not given through law (**14-15**)
3. But in light of faith, according to grace, to assure that all who are of

the same faith as Abraham might be heirs of the promise (**16-17**)
4. The kind of obedient faith illustrated by Abraham (**18-22**)
5. Abraham's justification by faith assures that we who believe in Him who raised Jesus from the dead shall find justification (**23-25**)

SUMMARY

Now that he has declared that God's righteousness is to be found in a system involving justification by faith and not by keeping the works of any law, Paul proceeds to provide evidence by referring to Abraham's example. In considering the justification of Abraham, Paul quotes Genesis 15:6 where it is stated that Abraham's faith was accounted to him for righteousness.

> **Romans 4:1-3 (NIV)** **¹What then shall we say that Abraham, our forefather, discovered in this matter? ²If, in fact, Abraham was justified by works, he had something to boast about—but not before God. ³What does the Scripture say? "Abraham believed God, and it was credited to him as righteousness."**

Abraham trusted in God, not in his own (forgiveness) expressed by David in Psalms 31:1,2.

> *Romans 4:4-8 (NIV)* *⁴Now when a man works, his wages are not credited to him as a gift, but as an obligation. ⁵However, to the man who does not work but trusts God who justifies the wicked, his faith is credited as righteousness. ⁶David says the same thing when he speaks of the blessedness of the man to whom God credits righteousness apart from works: ⁷"Blessed are they whose transgressions are forgiven, whose sins are covered. ⁸Blessed is the man whose sin the Lord will never count against him."*

To demonstrate further that God's righteousness by faith is offered to both Jew and Gentile, Paul again appeals to the example of Abraham. He reminds them that Abraham's faith was accounted for righteousness prior to receiving circumcision, which was in itself a seal of the righteousness of the faith he had while uncircumcised. Thus Abraham serves as a father of all who believe, whether circumcised or not.

> *Romans 4:9-12 (NIV)* *⁹Is this blessedness only for the circumcised, or also for the uncircumcised? We have been saying that Abraham's faith was credited to him as righteousness. ¹⁰Under what circumstances was it credited? Was it after he was circumcised, or before? It was not after, but before! ¹¹And he received the sign of circumcision, a seal of the righteousness that he had by faith while he was still uncircumcised. So then, he is the father of*

all who believe but have not been circumcised, in order that righteousness might be credited to them. 12And he is also the father of the circumcised who not only are circumcised but who also walk in the footsteps of the faith that our father Abraham had before he was circumcised.

Paul then reminds them that the promise that Abraham was to be "a father of many nations" was given in light of his faith, not through some law, so that the promise might be according to grace and sure to those who have the same kind of faith as Abraham.

Romans 4:13-17 (NIV) 13It was not through law that Abraham and his offspring received the promise that he would be heir of the world, but through the righteousness that comes by faith. 14For if those who live by law are heirs, faith has no value and the promise is worthless, 15because law brings wrath. And where there is no law there is no transgression. 16Therefore, the promise comes by faith, so that it may be by grace and may be guaranteed to all Abraham's offspring—not only to those who are of the law but also to those who are of the faith of Abraham. He is the father of us all. 17As it is written: "I have made you a father of many nations." He is our father in the sight of God, in whom he believed—the God who gives life to the dead and calls things that are not as though they were.

Finally, the nature of Abraham's obedient faith is illustrated.

> **Romans 4:18-22 (NIV)** **[18]Against all hope, Abraham in hope believed and so became the father of many nations, just as it had been said to him, "So shall your offspring be." [19]Without weakening in his faith, he faced the fact that his body was as good as dead—since he was about a hundred years old—and that Sarah's womb was also dead. [20]Yet he did not waver through unbelief regarding the promise of God, but was strengthened in his faith and gave glory to God, [21]being fully persuaded that God had power to do what he had promised. [22]This is why "it was credited to him as righteousness."**

With the explanation it was preserved to reassure us that we who have the same kind faith in God who raised Jesus will find our faith accounted for righteousness in the same way.

> **Romans 4:23-25 (NIV)** **[23]The words "it was credited to him" were written not for him alone, [24]but also for us, to whom God will credit righteousness—for us who believe in him who raised Jesus our Lord from the dead. [25]He was delivered over to death for our sins and was raised to life for our justification.**

REVIEW QUESTIONS FOR THE CHAPTER

1) List the main points of this chapter

_____

_____

2) How did Abraham attain righteousness? **(3-5)**

_____

_____

3) How does David describe the righteousness which is imputed to man? **(6-8)**

_____

_____

4) How is Abraham the father of the uncircumcised who possess faith? **(9-11)**

_____

_____

5) Based upon what was the promise made to Abraham? **(13)**

_____

_____

6) How did Abraham demonstrate his faith? **(19-21)**

_____

_____

7) For whose sake was the example of Abraham's faith written? **(23-24)**

_____

_____

Chapter Five

OBJECTIVES IN STUDYING THIS CHAPTER

1) To appreciate the blessings that accompany justification
2) To comprehend more fully the grace offered through Jesus Christ

OUTLINE

I. **THE BLESSINGS OF JUSTIFICATION** (1-11)

A. **PEACE WITH GOD** (1)

B. **ACCESS TO GRACE IN WHICH WE STAND** (2a)

C. REJOICING IN HOPE, EVEN IN TRIBULATION (2b-4)

1. Joy in anticipating God's glory (**2b**)
2. Joy in tribulation , knowing even it results in more hope (**3-4**)
3. For tribulation produces perseverance (**3b**)
4. And perseverance develops character (**4a**)
5. Such character gives one hope (**4b**)

D. GOD'S LOVE IN OUR HEARTS (5-8)

1. The assurance our hope will not be disappointed (**5a**)
2. Poured out by the Holy Spirit (**5b**)
3. Demonstrated by Christ's death while we were yet sinners (**6-8**)

E. SALVATION FROM GOD'S WRATH (9-11)

1. Through Jesus, just as we have been justified by His blood (**9**)
2. Saved by His life, just as we were reconciled by His death (**10**)
3. The basis for us to rejoice (**11**)

II. <u>COMPARING CHRIST WITH ADAM</u> (12-21)

A. ADAM AND THE CONSEQUENCE OF HIS ACTIONS (12-14)

1. Through Adam, sin entered the world, and death as a consequence (**12a**)
2. Thus death spread, for all sinned (**12b**)

3. From the time of Adam to Moses, death reigned, even over those who had not sinned like Adam did (**13-14**)

B. **ADAM AND CHRIST COMPARED (15-19)**
   1. Adam's offence brought many deaths, Christ's grace abounds even more (**15**)
   2. One offence produced the judgment of condemnation, but may offenses produced the free gift of justification (**16**)
   3. By Adam's offense death reigns, but those who receive the gift of righteousness will reign in life through Christ (**17**)
   4. Summary (**18-19**)
   5. Through Adam's offense judgment came to all men, resulting in condemnation (**18a**)
   6. Through Christ's act grace came to all, resulting in justification of life (**18b**)
   7. By Adam's disobedience many were made sinners (**19a**)
   8. By Christ's obedience many will be made righteous (**19b**)

C. **THE RELATIONSHIP OF LAW, SIN AND GRACE (20-21)**
   1. Law entered that sin might abound, but grace abounds much more (**20**)

2. Just as sin reigned in death, so grace reigns through righteousness to eternal life through Christ (**21**)

SUMMARY

Having substantiated his thesis of "justification by faith" with evidence from the Old Testament, Paul now discusses the blessings of such justification. First, there is peace with God.

Romans 5:1(NIV) Therefore, since we have been justified through faith, we have peace with God through our Lord Jesus Christ,

Second, we have access to grace in which we stand.

Romans 5:2a (NIV) through whom we have gained access by faith into this grace in which we now stand.

Third, there is cause for rejoicing in hope, so that we can glory even in tribulations.

Romans 5:2b-4 (NIV) And we rejoice in the hope of the glory of God. ³Not only so, but we also rejoice in our sufferings, because we know that suffering produces perseverance; ⁴perseverance, character; and character, hope.

Fourth, there is God's love which He first demonstrated with the gift of His Son.

> *Romans 5:5-8 (NIV) ⁵And hope does not disappoint us, because God has poured out his love into our hearts by the Holy Spirit, whom he has given us. ⁶You see, at just the right time, when we were still powerless, Christ died for the ungodly. ⁷Very rarely will anyone die for a righteous man, though for a good man someone might possibly dare to die. ⁸But God demonstrates his own love for us in this: While we were still sinners, Christ died for us.*

Finally, there is salvation from God's wrath.

> *Romans 5:9 (NIV) Since we have now been justified by his blood, how much more shall we be saved from God's wrath through him!*

All of this is made possible when we are reconciled to God through the death of His son and should be the basis for endless rejoicing.

> *Romans 5:10-11 (NIV) ¹⁰For if, when we were God's enemies, we were reconciled to him through the death of his Son, how much more, having been reconciled, shall we be saved through his life! ¹¹Not only is this so, but we also rejoice in God through our Lord Jesus Christ, through whom we have now received reconciliation.*

To explain further the way in which salvation is made possible, Paul compares Christ to Adam.

Through one man, Adam, sin and death entered the world, and the consequences have led to the death of many. In a similar way, through one man, Christ, many may now become righteous. Through Jesus' death on the cross, justification is made possible for many.

> ***Romans 5:12-19 (NIV)** **12**Therefore, just as sin entered the world through one man, and death through sin, and in this way death came to all men, because all sinned— **13**for before the law was given, sin was in the world. But sin is not taken into account when there is no law. **14**Nevertheless, death reigned from the time of Adam to the time of Moses, even over those who did not sin by breaking a command, as did Adam, who was a pattern of the one to come. **15**But the gift is not like the trespass. For if the many died by the trespass of the one man, how much more did God's grace and the gift that came by the grace of the one man, Jesus Christ, overflow to the many! **16**Again, the gift of God is not like the result of the one man's sin: The judgment followed one sin and brought condemnation, but the gift followed many trespasses and brought justification. **17**For if, by the trespass of the one man, death reigned through that one man, how much more will those who receive God's abundant provision of grace and of the gift of righteousness reign in life through the one man, Jesus Christ. **18**Consequently, just as the result of one*

trespass was condemnation for all men, so also the result of one act of righteousness was justification that brings life for all men. ¹⁹For just as through the disobedience of the one man the many were made sinners, so also through the obedience of the one man the many will be made righteous.

Upon comparing Christ with Adam, Paul briefly mentions that with the entering in of law sin abounded. But the increase of sin has been adequately answered by the grace offered in Jesus Christ.

Romans 5:20-21 (NIV) ²⁰The law was added so that the trespass might increase. But where sin increased, grace increased all the more, ²¹so that, just as sin reigned in death, so also grace might reign through righteousness to bring eternal life through Jesus Christ our Lord.

REVIEW QUESTIONS FOR THE CHAPTER

1) List the main points of this chapter

_____

_____

2) Name some benefits we enjoy as the result of justification (**1-2**)

_____

_____

3) Why can Christians rejoice even in the middle of trials? (**3-5**)

_____

_____

4) How did God demonstrate His love for us? (**6-8**)

_____

_____

5) What in addition to Jesus' death is involved in our ultimate salvation? (**10**)

_____

_____

6) What was the consequence of Adam's sin upon all men? (**12**)

_____

_____

7) What comparison is made between Adam and Christ? (**12-19**)

_____

_____

8) Which has abounded more: sin, or grace? (**20**)

_____

_____

Chapter Six

OBJECTIVES IN STUDYING THIS CHAPTER

1) To understand what takes place in baptism
2) To appreciate the freedom from sin which we may now enjoy in Christ

OUTLINE

I. <u>WE ARE DEAD TO SIN!</u> (1-14)

   A. THROUGH BAPTISM WE DIED TO SIN (1-7)
      1. Shall we sin, that grace may abound? No, we died to sin! (**1-2**)
      2. In baptism we were buried into Christ's death (**3-4a**)

3. We should walk in newness of life, having been united together in the likeness of His death, crucified with Him, no longer slaves of sin, but freed from sin (**4b-7**)

B. DEAD TO SIN, ALIVE TO GOD (8-14)
1. Having died with Christ, we may live with Him over Whom death has no dominion (**8-10**)
2. Alive to God, we should not let sin reign in our bodies (**11-12**)
3. But rather present our bodies as instruments of righteousness, for we are under grace (**13-14**)

II. <u>WE SHOULD BE SLAVES TO GOD!</u> (15-23)

A. WE BECOME SLAVES TO WHOM WE OBEY (15-18)
1. Either of sin to death, or of obedience to righteousness (**15-16**)
2. Through obedience to God's Word, those who were slaves of sin become slaves of righteousness (**17-18**)

B. THE MOTIVATION FOR SERVING GOD (19-23)
1. Serving righteousness produces holiness (**19**)
2. Serving sin produces death (**20-21**)

3. Serving God produces the fruit of holiness, and in the end, eternal life (**22**)
4. The wages of sin is death, but God gives the gift of eternal life in Christ Jesus our Lord (**23**)

SUMMARY

In chapter five, Paul made the statement "where sin abounded, grace abounded much more" (5:20). Aware that some readers might misconstrue what he said, Paul quickly points out that grace is no excuse to sin since through grace, they have died to sin.

> *Romans 6:1-2 (NIV)* ¹*What shall we say, then? Shall we go on sinning so that grace may increase? ²By no means! We died to sin; how can we live in it any longer?*

To emphasize this, he reminds them of their baptism into Christ, in which they experienced a burial into the death of Christ and rose to walk in newness of life, having died to sin.

> *Romans 6:3-7 (NIV)* ³*Or don't you know that all of us who were baptized into Christ Jesus were baptized into his death? ⁴We were therefore buried with him through baptism into death in order that, just as Christ was raised from the dead through the glory of the Father, we too may live a new life. ⁵If we have been united with him like this in his*

death, we will certainly also be united with him in his resurrection. ⁶For we know that our old self was crucified with him so that the body of sin might be done away with, that we should no longer be slaves to sin—⁷because anyone who has died has been freed from sin.

Dead to sin, they are now free to live as instruments of righteousness for God.

Romans 6:8-14 (NIV) ⁸Now if we died with Christ, we believe that we will also live with him. ⁹For we know that since Christ was raised from the dead, he cannot die again; death no longer has mastery over him. ¹⁰The death he died, he died to sin once for all; but the life he lives, he lives to God. ¹¹In the same way, count yourselves dead to sin but alive to God in Christ Jesus. ¹²Therefore do not let sin reign in your mortal body so that you obey its evil desires. ¹³Do not offer the parts of your body to sin, as instruments of wickedness, but rather offer yourselves to God, as those who have been brought from death to life; and offer the parts of your body to him as instruments of righteousness. ¹⁴For sin shall not be your master, because you are not under law, but under grace.

Another reason not to continue in sin is explained in terms of servitude. We become slaves to that which we obey, either sin or God.

> *Romans 6:15-16 (NIV) ⁱ⁵What then? Shall we sin because we are not under law but under grace? By no means! ¹⁶Don't you know that when you offer yourselves to someone to obey him as slaves, you are slaves to the one whom you obey—whether you are slaves to sin, which leads to death, or to obedience, which leads to righteousness?*

But Paul is grateful that the Romans had begun to obey God and were free to become His servants.

> *Romans 6:17-18 (NIV) ¹⁷But thanks be to God that, though you used to be slaves to sin, you wholeheartedly obeyed the form of teaching to which you were entrusted. ¹⁸You have been set free from sin and have become slaves to righteousness.*

How important it is that they continue to do so is to be seen in the outcome of serving sin contrasted to serving God. Serving sin earns death, but in serving God one receives the gift of eternal life in Christ Jesus!

> *Romans 6:19-23 (NIV) ¹⁹I put this in human terms because you are weak in your natural selves. Just as you used to offer the parts of your body in slavery to impurity and to ever-increasing wickedness, so now offer them in slavery to righteousness leading to holiness. ²⁰When you were slaves to sin, you were free from the control of righteousness. ²¹What*

benefit did you reap at that time from the things you are now ashamed of? Those things result in death! ²²But now that you have been set free from sin and have become slaves to God, the benefit you reap leads to holiness, and the result is eternal life. ²³For the wages of sin is death, but the gift of God is eternal life in Christ Jesus our Lord.

REVIEW QUESTIONS FOR THE CHAPTER

1) List the main points of this chapter
_____
_____

2) Why are Christians not to continue in sin? **(2)**
_____
_____

3) What happens when one is baptized into Christ? **(3-7)**
_____
_____

4) How should we present the members of our bodies? **(13)**
_____
_____

5) Why does sin no longer have dominion over the Christian? **(14)**
_____
_____

6) What was necessary to become free from sin? **(17-18)**

_____

_____

7) What is the result of presenting your members as slaves to righteousness? **(19)**

_____

_____

8) What three steps are described that eventually lead to eternal life? **(22)**

_____

_____

9) What is the just payment for sin? But what does God give us in Christ? **(23)**

_____

_____

Chapter Seven

OBJECTIVES IN STUDYING THIS CHAPTER

1) To understand the Jewish Christian's relationship to the Law of Moses
2) To comprehend the dilemma one faces without Jesus Christ

OUTLINE

I. **JEWISH BELIEVERS AND THE LAW (1-6)**

A. **A PARALLEL TO BEING RELEASED FORM MARRIAGE (1-3)**
   1. Law has dominion over those who live under it (**1**)
   2. As illustrated by a woman who is married to a man (**2-3**)

B. THEY HAVE DIED TO THE LAW (4-6)
   1. So they can be married to Christ (**4**)
   2. So they can serve in newness of the Spirit, far superior to serving in the oldness of the letter (**5-6**)

II. LIMITATIONS OF THE LAW (7-25)

A. THE LAW IS HOLY AND JUST AND GOOD (7-12)
   1. The Law is not sin, but rather makes known sin (**7**)
   2. But sin takes occasion by the commandment to lead one to death (**8-12**)

B. THE LAW CANNOT SAVE ONE FROM SIN (13-25)
   1. The problem is not law, but sin (**13**)
   2. The law is spiritual, but man is carnal and sold under sin (**14**)
   3. Though one may desire good and hate evil, one is still enslaved by sin (**15-23**)
   4. Deliverance comes only from God, through Jesus Christ (**24-25**

SUMMARY

Paul has just completed discussing how being baptized into Christ makes us dead to sin and free to present our bodies as instruments of righteousness unto holiness. For the benefit of his Jewish readers (those who know the Law), he now carries the concept of death and freedom one step further: the Jewish believers become dead to the Law that they might be joined to Christ. He illustrates his point by referring to the marital relationship. The result of being freed from the Law is that they might "serve in the newness of the Spirit and not in the oldness of the letter."

***Romans 7:1-6 (NIV)** **¹Do you not know, brothers—for I am speaking to men who know the law—that the law has authority over a man only as long as he lives? ²For example, by law a married woman is bound to her husband as long as he is alive, but if her husband dies, she is released from the law of marriage. ³So then, if she marries another man while her husband is still alive, she is called an adulteress. But if her husband dies, she is released from that law and is not an adulteress, even though she marries another man. ⁴So, my brothers, you also died to the law through the body of Christ, that you might belong to another, to him who was raised from the dead, in order that we might bear fruit to God. ⁵For when we were controlled by the sinful nature, the sinful passions aroused by the law were at work in our bodies, so that we bore fruit for death. ⁶But now, by dying to what once bound us, we have been released from the law so that we serve in the new way of the Spirit, and not in the old way of the written code.*

Lest his Jewish readers think he is implying that the Law was sinful, Paul is quick to dispel that notion. The Law, he says, is "holy and just and good." The problem is that the Law only makes known that which is sinful, but sin took opportunity by the commandment to produce evil desire and deceived him, resulting in death.

> ***Romans 7:7-12 (NIV)** ⁷What shall we say, then? Is the law sin? Certainly not! Indeed I would not have known what sin was except through the law. For I would not have known what coveting really was if the law had not said, "Do not covet." ⁸But sin, seizing the opportunity afforded by the commandment, produced in me every kind of covetous desire. For apart from law, sin is dead. ⁹Once I was alive apart from law; but when the commandment came, sin sprang to life and I died. ¹⁰I found that the very commandment that was intended to bring life actually brought death. ¹¹For sin, seizing the opportunity afforded by the commandment, deceived me, and through the commandment put me to death. ¹²So then, the law is holy, and the commandment is holy, righteous and good.*

To further illustrate his point, Paul pictures himself as man under the law who finds himself in a terrible dilemma. With his mind he knows that which is good and wants to do it. He also knows that which is evil and wants to avoid that. But he finds a "law" (or principle) in his flesh which wins over the desire of the mind.

> **Romans 7:13-23 (NIV)** **¹³Did that which is good, then, become death to me? By no means! But in order that sin might be recognized as sin, it produced death in me through what was good, so that through the commandment sin might become utterly sinful. ¹⁴We know that the law is spiritual; but I am unspiritual, sold as a slave to sin. ¹⁵I do not understand what I do. For what I want to do I do not do, but what I hate I do. ¹⁶And if I do what I do not want to do, I agree that the law is good. ¹⁷As it is, it is no longer I myself who do it, but it is sin living in me. ¹⁸I know that nothing good lives in me, that is, in my sinful nature. For I have the desire to do what is good, but I cannot carry it out. ¹⁹For what I do is not the good I want to do; no, the evil I do not want to do—this I keep on doing. ²⁰Now if I do what I do not want to do, it is no longer I who do it, but it is sin living in me that does it. ²¹So I find this law at work: When I want to do good, evil is right there with me. ²²For in my inner being I delight in God's law; ²³but I see another law at work in the members of my body, waging war against the law of my mind and making me a prisoner of the law of sin at work within my members.**

As a prisoner he cries out for freedom. Is there no hope? Yes! God provides the solution through His

Son Jesus Christ, upon which Paul will elaborate in chapter eight.

> **Romans 7:24-25 (NIV)** **24What a wretched man I am! Who will rescue me from this body of death? 25Thanks be to God—through Jesus Christ our Lord! So then, I myself in my mind am a slave to God's law, but in the sinful nature a slave to the law of sin.**

REVIEW QUESTIONS FOR THE CHAPTER

1) List the main points of this chapter

_____

_____

2) Who is Paul speaking to in this chapter? **(1)**

_____

_____

3) What example is given to show their relationship to the Law? **(2-3)**

_____

_____

4) What is their relationship to the Law when joined to the body of Christ? **(4-6)**

_____

_____

5) How do we know the Law referred to is the Ten Commandments? **(7)**

_____

_____

6) What the Law responsible for death? If not, what was? **(13)**

_____

_____

7) What dilemma does one face in trying to keep the Law? **(15-21)**

_____

_____

8) What is the end result of this dilemma? **(23)**

_____

_____

9) Where can one find freedom from this dilemma? **(24-25)**

_____

_____

Chapter Eight

OBJECTIVES IN STUDYING THIS CHAPTER

1) To appreciate the place the Holy Spirit has in the lives of Christians
2) To notice the power to overcome sin which is available in Christ
3) To realize the extent of God's love toward us.

OUTLINE

I. <u>**IN CHRIST THERE IS FREEDOM FROM SIN**</u> **(1-17)**

    A. FREEDOM FROM THE CONDEMNATION OF SIN (1-4)
        1. Available to those in Christ, made possible by the law of the Spirit of life **(1-2)**

2. An accomplishment not attained by the Law, but by the death of Christ (**3-4**)

B. FREEDOM FORM THE POWER OF SIN (5-17)
1. To those who set their minds on the things of the Spirit, not the flesh, pleasing God. (**5-8**)
2. To those who have the indwelling Holy Spirit (**9-11**)
3. To those who by the Spirit put to death the deeds of the body (**12-13**)
4. To those thus led, who are the children of God and joint heirs with Christ (**14-17**)

II. <u>BLESSINGS OF BEING CHILDREN OF GOD</u> (18-39)

A. THE GLORY TO BE REVEALED IN US (18-25)
1. Present sufferings don't even compare (**18**)
2. The whole creation eagerly awaits for the revealing and glorious liberty of the children of God (**19-22**)
3. We also eagerly wait with perseverance for this hope (**23-25**)

B. THE HELP OF THE HOLY SPIRIT (26-27)
1. Helps in our weakness as we pray (**26a**)
2. By interceding for us as we pray (**26b-27**)

C. ALL THINGS WORKING TOGETHER FOR GOOD (28-30)
1. For those who love God, called according to His purpose (**28**)
2. For such, whom God foreknew, He will carry out His ultimate purpose (**29-30**)

D. GOD'S LOVE TOWARD HIS ELECT (31-39)
1. God, who spared not His own Son, is on our side (**31-33**)
2. Christ, who died for us, now intercedes for us at God's right hand (**34**)
3. Through such love, we are more than conquerors over all things (**35-39**

SUMMARY

In chapter seven, Paul described the dilemma of a man who becomes a prisoner of the law of sin which is in the members of his body. In the last few verses, Paul made reference to the hope of liberation made possible by God through Jesus Christ. In this chapter, Paul amplifies on the freedom from sin found in Christ.

First, for those in Christ who are walking according to the Spirit, there is no condemnation for sin, for the death of Christ for sin has set us free from the law of sin and death by fulfilling the requirement of the law.

Romans 8:1-4 (NIV) ¹*Therefore, there is now no condemnation for those who are in Christ*

Jesus, ²because through Christ Jesus the law of the Spirit of life set me free from the law of sin and death. ³For what the law was powerless to do in that it was weakened by the sinful nature, God did by sending his own Son in the likeness of sinful man to be a sin offering. And so he condemned sin in sinful man, ⁴in order that the righteous requirements of the law might be fully met in us, who do not live according to the sinful nature but according to the Spirit.

Second, by setting our minds on the things of the Spirit and not the flesh, we are able to enjoy life and peace, pleasing God.

Romans 8:5-8 (NIV)   ⁵Those who live according to the sinful nature have their minds set on what that nature desires; but those who live in accordance with the Spirit have their minds set on what the Spirit desires. ⁶The mind of sinful man is death, but the mind controlled by the Spirit is life and peace; ⁷the sinful mind is hostile to God. It does not submit to God's law, nor can it do so. ⁸Those controlled by the sinful nature cannot please God.

And third, we now enjoy the indwelling of the Spirit of God, by whom we can put to death the deeds of the body and enjoy both present and future blessings as the children of God.

Romans 8:9-17 (NIV) ⁹You, however, are controlled not by the sinful nature but by the Spirit, if the Spirit of God lives in you. And if anyone does not have the Spirit of Christ, he does not belong to Christ. ¹⁰But if Christ is in you, your body is dead because of sin, yet your spirit is alive because of righteousness. ¹¹And if the Spirit of him who raised Jesus from the dead is living in you, he who raised Christ from the dead will also give life to your mortal bodies through his Spirit, who lives in you. ¹²Therefore, brothers, we have an obligation—but it is not to the sinful nature, to live according to it. ¹³For if you live according to the sinful nature, you will die; but if by the Spirit you put to death the misdeeds of the body, you will live, ¹⁴because those who are led by the Spirit of God are sons of God. ¹⁵For you did not receive a spirit that makes you a slave again to fear, but you received the Spirit of sonship. And by him we cry, "Abba, Father." ¹⁶The Spirit himself testifies with our spirit that we are God's children. ¹⁷Now if we are children, then we are heirs—heirs of God and co-heirs with Christ, if indeed we share in his sufferings in order that we may also share in his glory.

The blessings of being God's children are enlarged upon in the rest of the chapter. Our present sufferings mean nothing in view of our ultimate redemption and revealing for which we eagerly and patiently wait.

Romans 8:18-25 (NIV) [18]I consider that our present sufferings are not worth comparing with the glory that will be revealed in us. [19]The creation waits in eager expectation for the sons of God to be revealed. [20]For the creation was subjected to frustration, not by its own choice, but by the will of the one who subjected it, in hope [21]that the creation itself will be liberated from its bondage to decay and brought into the glorious freedom of the children of God. [22]We know that the whole creation has been groaning as in the pains of childbirth right up to the present time. [23]Not only so, but we ourselves, who have the firstfruits of the Spirit, groan inwardly as we wait eagerly for our adoption as sons, the redemption of our bodies. [24]For in this hope we were saved. But hope that is seen is no hope at all. Who hopes for what he already has? [25]But if we hope for what we do not yet have, we wait for it patiently.

We have the privilege of the Holy Spirit and Jesus interceding for us when we pray, which assures that all things will work together for the good for those called according to God's purpose.

Romans 8:26-30 (NIV) [26]In the same way, the Spirit helps us in our weakness. We do not know what we ought to pray for, but the Spirit himself intercedes for us with groans that words cannot express. [27]And he who searches our hearts knows the mind of the Spirit, because the Spirit intercedes for the saints in accordance with God's will. ²⁸And we know that in all things God works for the good of those who love him, who have been called according to his purpose. ²⁹For those God foreknew he also predestined to be conformed to the likeness of his Son, that he might be the firstborn among many brothers. ³⁰And those he predestined, he also called; those he called, he also justified; those he justified, he also glorified.

Finally, as God's elect we have the assurance that nothing can tear us away from God's love, and that in all things we are more than conquerors through Him who loved us.

Romans 8:31-39 (NIV) ³¹What, then, shall we say in response to this? If God is for us, who can be against us? ³²He who did not spare his own Son, but gave him up for us all—how will he not also, along with him, graciously give us all things? ³³Who will bring any charge against those whom God has chosen? It is God who justifies. ³⁴Who is he that condemns? Christ Jesus, who died— more than that, who was raised to life—is at the right hand of God and is also interceding for us. ³⁵Who shall separate us from the love of Christ? Shall trouble or hardship or persecution or famine or nakedness or danger or sword? ³⁶As it is written: "For your sake we face death all day long; we are considered as sheep to be slaughtered." ³⁷No, in all these things we are more than conquerors through him who loved us. ³⁸For I am convinced that neither death nor life, neither angels nor demons, neither the present nor the future, nor any powers, ³⁹neither height nor depth, nor anything else in all creation, will be able to separate us from the love of God that is in Christ Jesus our Lord.

REVIEW QUESTIONS FOR THE CHAPTER

1) List the main points of this chapter

_____

_____

2) What is the main difference between the "law of Moses" and the "law of the Spirit of life?" **(2-4)**

_____

_____

3) What is the result of setting your mind on the things of the flesh? On the things of the Spirit? **(6)**

_____

_____

4) Do the Scriptures teach that the Holy Spirit dwells in the Christian? **(9-11)**

_____

_____

5) How can we assure that we will continue to live spiritually? (**13**)

_____

_____

6) List briefly the blessings of being the children of God (**14-39**)

_____

_____

Chapter Nine

OBJECTIVES IN STUDYING THIS CHAPTER

1) To appreciate why and how God could choose to reject the nation of Israel (except for a remnant) and accept people from among the Gentiles.

OUTLINE

I. **PAUL'S CONCERN FOR HIS BRETHREN OF ISRAEL** (1-5)

A. HIS GREAT CONCERN (1-3)
   1. His conscience and the Holy Spirit bear witness to his great sorrow and grief (**1-2**)
   2. He would even be willing to be cut off from Christ for their sakes (**3**)

B. **FOR ISRAEL, RECIPIENTS OF MANY BLESSINGS (4-5)**
   1. Including the covenants, the Law, the promises (**4**)
   2. Of whom are the patriarchs, and of course, Christ Himself (**5**)

II. **THE TRUE CHILDREN OF GOD (6-29)**

A. **ARE CHILDREN OF PROMISE, NOT CHILDREN OF FLESH (6-13)**
   1. They are not all Israel who have descended from Israel (**6**)
   2. As illustrated with Isaac and Ishmael, Jacob and Esau (**7-13**)
   3. According to God's purpose, whose choice was not based upon works (**11**)

B. **ARE THE OBJECTS OF GOD'S MERCY (14-23)**
   1. Possible only through His Mercy (**14-16**)
   2. Just as Pharaoh was the object of His Wrath (**17-18**)
   3. God's right to choose the objects of His mercy and His wrath (**19-23**)

C. **ARE OF BOTH THE JEWS AND THE GENTILES (24-29)**
   1. Not of Jews only, as foretold by Hosea (**24-26**)
   2. But only a remnant of Israel, as foretold by Isaiah (**27-29**)

III. THE BASIS OF GOD'S CHOICE: FAITH vs. NO FAITH (30-33)

A. FOR THE GENTILES (30)
1. Though they had not actively been looking for it (**30a**)
2. Yet many have attained righteousness through faith (**30b**)

B. FOR ISRAEL (31-33)
1. Though diligent for the Law, did not have the attitude of faith (**31-32a**)
2. And therefore stumbled over Christ, as foretold by Isaiah (**32b-33**)

SUMMARY

With the conclusion of chapter eight, Paul has completed his description of how God's righteousness was manifested in Christ, and the results of such justification. However, some of Paul's readers may have received the impression that God's plan of saving man in Christ apart from the Law (**3:21-22**) implies that God has rejected His people of Israel and the promises made to them. In chapters nine through eleven, Paul explains that God has not rejected His people.

Paul first expresses his own concern for his fellow Israelites.

Romans 9:1-2 (NIV) ¹I speak the truth in Christ—I am not lying, my conscience confirms it in the Holy Spirit— ²I have great sorrow and unceasing anguish in my heart.

If it would do any good, Paul would gladly be condemned in order to save his brethren who had been the recipients of so many blessings.

Romans 9:3 (NIV) For I could wish that I myself were cursed and cut off from Christ for the sake of my brothers, those of my own race,

But Paul quickly states that God's promises had not failed.

Romans 9:4-5 (NIV) ⁴the people of Israel. Theirs is the adoption as sons; theirs the divine glory, the covenants, the receiving of the law, the temple worship and the promises. ⁵Theirs are the patriarchs, and from them is traced the human ancestry of Christ, who is God over all, forever praised! Amen.

He reminds them that true Israel is not simply the physical descendants of Israel, any more than the promises to Abraham were to be carried out through all of Abraham's descendants just because they are his physical descendants. Rather, it depends upon what God has chosen according to His Divine purpose. This is illustrated by contrasting what the Scriptures reveal about

Isaac and Ishmael, and then about Jacob and Esau.

> **Romans 9:6-13 (NIV)** **⁶It is not as though God's word had failed. For not all who are descended from Israel are Israel. ⁷Nor because they are his descendants are they all Abraham's children. On the contrary, "It is through Isaac that your offspring will be reckoned." ⁸In other words, it is not the natural children who are God's children, but it is the children of the promise who are regarded as Abraham's offspring. ⁹For this was how the promise was stated: "At the appointed time I will return, and Sarah will have a son." ¹⁰Not only that, but Rebekah's children had one and the same father, our father Isaac. ¹¹Yet, before the twins were born or had done anything good or bad—in order that God's purpose in election might stand: ¹²not by works but by him who calls— she was told, "The older will serve the younger." ¹³Just as it is written: "Jacob I loved, but Esau I hated."**

He reminds them that God has made such a distinction is illustrated further with the example of Pharaoh, where God chose to show mercy to some while He hardened others [who had already persistently rejected God's mercy].

> **Romans 9:14-18 (NIV)** **¹⁴What then shall we say? Is God unjust? Not at all! ¹⁵For he says to Moses, "I will have mercy on whom I have**

mercy, and I will have compassion on whom I have compassion." ¹⁶It does not, therefore, depend on man's desire or effort, but on God's mercy. ¹⁷For the Scripture says to Pharaoh: "I raised you up for this very purpose, that I might display my power in you and that my name might be proclaimed in all the earth." ¹⁸Therefore God has mercy on whom he wants to have mercy, and he hardens whom he wants to harden.

He reminds them that God has the right to make such choices is His as the potter over the clay.

Romans 9:19-21 (NIV) ¹⁹One of you will say to me: "Then why does God still blame us? For who resists his will?" ²⁰But who are you, O man, to talk back to God? "Shall what is formed say to him who formed it, 'Why did you make me like this?' " ²¹Does not the potter have the right to make out of the same lump of clay some pottery for noble purposes and some for common use?

So God chose to endure "vessels of wrath" with much longsuffering, that He might make known His glorious riches to "vessels of mercy" [a point expanded upon further in chapter eleven].

Romans 9:22-23 (NIV) ²²What if God, choosing to show his wrath and make his power known, bore with great patience the objects of his wrath—prepared for

> *destruction? ²³What if he did this to make the riches of his glory known to the objects of his mercy, whom he prepared in advance for glory—*

And who are these "vessels of mercy?" They consist of Gentiles, and a remnant of Israel, as foretold by Hosea and Isaiah.

> *Romans 9:24-29 (NIV) ²⁴even us, whom he also called, not only from the Jews but also from the Gentiles? ²⁵As he says in Hosea: "I will call them 'my people' who are not my people; and I will call her 'my loved one' who is not my loved one," ²⁶and, "It will happen that in the very place where it was said to them, 'You are not my people,' they will be called 'sons of the living God.' " ²⁷Isaiah cries out concerning Israel: "Though the number of the Israelites be like the sand by the sea, only the remnant will be saved. ²⁸For the Lord will carry out his sentence on earth with speed and finality." ²⁹It is just as Isaiah said previously: "Unless the Lord Almighty had left us descendants, we would have become like Sodom, we would have been like Gomorrah."*

Paul's conclusion? That God's words of promise were not just to the fleshly descendants of Abraham (as the Jews would have it), but to the faithful remnant of Israel and to the Gentiles who accepted the righteousness which is by faith. The only reason any of the Israelites were rejected by

God was because of their rejection of the Messiah, even as Isaiah foretold.

Romans 9:30-33 (NIV) ³⁰What then shall we say? That the Gentiles, who did not pursue righteousness, have obtained it, a righteousness that is by faith; ³¹but Israel, who pursued a law of righteousness, has not attained it. ³²Why not? Because they pursued it not by faith but as if it were by works. They stumbled over the "stumbling stone." ³³As it is written: "See, I lay in Zion a stone that causes men to stumble and a rock that makes them fall, and the one who trusts in him will never be put to shame."

REVIEW QUESTIONS FOR THE CHAPTER

1) List the main points of this chapter

_____

_____

2) How much love did Paul have for the nation of Israel? (**2-3**)

_____

_____

3) Who are the true children of God? (**8**)

_____

_____

4) What does God have the right to do? (**18**)

_____

_____

5) What O.T. prophet foretold that Gentiles would be a part of the people of God? (**25-26**)

_____

_____

6) What did Isaiah say would happen to the nation of Israel (**27**)

_____

_____

7) Why are Gentiles among the saved? (**30**)

_____

_____

8) Why are some Israelites going to be lost? (**31-33**)

_____

_____

Chapter Ten

OBJECTIVES IN STUDYING THIS CHAPTER

1) To see the importance of combining zeal with knowledge
2) To understand that Israel had plenty of opportunity to heed the gospel of Christ, but for the most part, had rejected it.

OUTLINE

I. ISRAEL'S REFUSAL OF GOD'S RIGHTEOUSNESS (1-15)

  A. PAUL'S EXPRESSION OF CONCERN FOR ISRAEL (1-4)
      1. That Israel be saved, for they have zeal but not knowledge (**1-2**).

2. Through ignorance, they seek to save themselves by the Law, and do not submit to God's righteousness in Christ which brings an end to the Law (**3-4**)

B. RIGHTEOUSNESS OF THE LAW vs. RIGHTEOUSNESS BY FAITH IN CHRIST (5-15)
1. Righteousness of the Law as defined by Moses (**5**)
2. Righteousness by faith as defined by Paul (**6-15**)
3. Involves the mouth and the heart (**6-8**)
4. Involves confessing Jesus and believing in His resurrection (**9-10**)
5. Offered to all who believe and call on Him (**11-13**)
6. Accomplished though the medium of preaching (**14-15**)

II. ISRAEL'S NEGLECT OF THE GOSPEL (16-21)

A. NOT ALL OBEYED THE GOSPEL (16-18)
1. As Isaiah predicted (**16**)
2. Even though they had ample opportunity (**17-18**)

B. THEIR NEGLECT, AND THE GENTILES RECEPTION, FORESEEN BY SCRIPTURES (19-21)
1. As spoken by Moses (**19**)
2. As spoken by Isaiah (**20-21**)

SUMMARY

As Paul continues to explain God's dealings with the nation of Israel, he repeats his expression of love towards them.

> *Romans 10: 1 (NIV)   Brothers, my heart's desire and prayer to God for the Israelites is that they may be saved.*

Though as a nation they had plenty of zeal, unfortunately, their zeal was not according to knowledge.

> *Romans 10:2 (NIV) For I can testify about them that they are zealous for God, but their zeal is not based on knowledge.*

Thus they rejected the righteousness of God while trying to establish their own righteousness through the Law of Moses. But Paul explains that Christ is the fulfillment of the Law and has brought it to an end.

> *Romans 10:3-4 (NIV)   ³Since they did not know the righteousness that comes from God and sought to establish their own, they did not submit to God's righteousness. ⁴Christ is the end of the law so that there may be righteousness for everyone who believes.*

The righteousness God now offers is based upon faith in Christ, not keeping the Law. It involves not the accomplishment of some great feat (like ascending to heaven or descending to hell), but such things as confessing Jesus as Lord and believing that God raised Him from the dead.

> **Romans 10:5-10 (NIV)** **⁵Moses describes in this way the righteousness that is by the law: "The man who does these things will live by them." ⁶But the righteousness that is by faith says: "Do not say in your heart, 'Who will ascend into heaven?'" (that is, to bring Christ down) ⁷"or 'Who will descend into the deep?'" (that is, to bring Christ up from the dead). ⁸But what does it say? "The word is near you; it is in your mouth and in your heart," that is, the word of faith we are proclaiming: ⁹That if you confess with your mouth, "Jesus is Lord," and believe in your heart that God raised him from the dead, you will be saved. ¹⁰For it is with your heart that you believe and are justified, and it is with your mouth that you confess and are saved.**

As foretold by Scripture, it is offered to all, both Jew and Gentile.

> **Romans 10:11-13 (NIV)** **¹¹As the Scripture says, "Anyone who trusts in him will never be put to shame." ¹²For there is no difference between Jew and Gentile—the same Lord is Lord of all and richly blesses all who call on him, ¹³for, "Everyone who calls on the name of the Lord will be saved."**

And it is offered through the medium of preaching the Word.

> **Romans 10:14-15 (NIV)** **¹⁴How, then, can they call on the one they have not believed in? And how can they believe in the one of whom they have not heard? And how can they hear without someone preaching to them? ¹⁵And how can they preach unless they are sent? As it is written, "How beautiful are the feet of those who bring good news!"**

The problem with the nation of Israel, then, is that not all of them received the gospel message, even when they had ample opportunity.

> **Romans 10:16-18 (NIV)** **¹⁶But not all the Israelites accepted the good news. For Isaiah says, "Lord, who has believed our message?" ¹⁷Consequently, faith comes from hearing the message, and the message is heard through the word of Christ. ¹⁸But I ask: Did they not hear? Of course they did: "Their voice has gone out into all the earth, their words to the ends of the world."**

But as Moses predicted, the day would come when God would provoke Israel to jealousy by another people, who Isaiah said did not seek God yet found Him, while Israel was constantly rebelling against Him.

> **Romans 10:19-21 (NIV)** **¹⁹Again I ask: Did Israel not understand? First, Moses says, "I**

will make you envious by those who are not a nation; I will make you angry by a nation that has no understanding." [20]And Isaiah boldly says, "I was found by those who did not seek me; I revealed myself to those who did not ask for me." [21]But concerning Israel he says, "All day long I have held out my hands to a disobedient and obstinate people."

REVIEW QUESTIONS FOR THE CHAPTER

1) List the main points of this chapter

_____

_____

2) What was Paul's prayer in behalf of the nation of Israel? **(1)**

_____

_____

3) What was good about them? What was wrong with them **(2)**

_____

_____

4) Why was Israel not submitting to the righteousness of God? **(3)**

_____

_____

5) What should one confess? What should one believe? **(9-10)**

_____

_____

6) For whom is righteousness by faith intended? **(11-13)**

_____

_____

7) What begins the process which finally enables one to call upon the Lord? **(14-15)**

_____

_____

8) How does one come to have faith? **(17)**

_____

_____

9) Did the Jews have opportunity to call upon the Lord? **(18)**

_____

_____

10) How did God say He was going to make His people jealous? **(19-20)**

_____

_____

Chapter Eleven

OBJECTIVES IN STUDYING THIS CHAPTER

1) To understand how God has not totally rejected His people of Israel
2) To see the possibility of apostasy for us today
3) To understand Paul's summary conclusion for this section (**chs. 9-11**)

OUTLINE

I. <u>GOD HAS NOT TOTALLY REJECTED ISRAEL</u> (1-10)

    A. EVIDENCE SUPPORTING THIS (1-6)
        1. Paul himself (**1**)
        2. There is a remnant, just as in the days of Elijah (**2-5a**)

3. A remnant according to grace, not works (**5b-6**)

B. **BUT MANY HAVE BEEN HARDENED (7-10)**
   1. An "elect" have been saved, the rest were hardened (**7**)
   2. This "hardening" foretold by Scriptures (**8-10**)

II. <u>**HARDENING OF ISRAEL TO BENEFIT ISRAEL**</u> **(11-32)**

A. **THE JEWISH STUMBLING AND GENTILE CONNECTION (11-16)**
   1. Salvation to the Gentiles an incentive for the Jews to repent (**11-12**)
   2. This is one reason why Paul magnified his ministry to the Gentiles (**13-16**)

B. **WORDS OF WARNING AGAINST GENTILE CONCEIT (17-24)**
   1. Gentiles are but "wild branches" grafted in to the root (**17-18**)
   2. To replace "broken branches", true, but can just as easily be displaced and replaced (**19-24**).

C. **THE HARDENING AND BLESSING OF ISRAEL (25-32)**
   1. Hardening is partial, until the fullness of the Gentiles come in (**25**)
   2. In this way all Israel will be saved (**26-27**)

3. They may be enemies of the gospel, but they are beloved by God (**28**)
4. And they may obtain mercy just as the Gentiles did (**29-32**)

III   <u>**PAUL'S HYMN OF PRAISE TO GOD**</u> (33-36)

SUMMARY

Paul concluded chapter ten with a quotation from Isaiah describing the nation of Israel as "a disobedient and contrary people." Paul begins chapter eleven by giving several examples to show that despite this rebellion, God has not totally rejected His people.

> *Romans 11:1-6 (NIV) ¹I ask then: Did God reject his people? By no means! I am an Israelite myself, a descendant of Abraham, from the tribe of Benjamin. ²God did not reject his people, whom he foreknew. Don't you know what the Scripture says in the passage about Elijah—how he appealed to God against Israel: ³"Lord, they have killed your prophets and torn down your altars; I am the only one left, and they are trying to kill me"? ⁴And what was God's answer to him? "I have reserved for myself seven thousand who have not bowed the knee to Baal." ⁵So too, at the present time there is a remnant chosen by grace. ⁶And if by grace, then it is no longer by works; if it were, grace would no longer be grace.*

What God has done, however, is harden the hearts of the rebellious Israelites.

> **Romans 11:7-10 (NIV)** **⁷What then? What Israel sought so earnestly it did not obtain, but the elect did. The others were hardened, ⁸as it is written: "God gave them a spirit of stupor, eyes so that they could not see and ears so that they could not hear, to this very day." ⁹And David says: "May their table become a snare and a trap, a stumbling block and a retribution for them. ¹⁰May their eyes be darkened so they cannot see, and their backs be bent forever."**

But the outcome of this "hardening" led to salvation coming to the Gentiles, which in turn God was using to provoke Israel to jealousy in an attempt to win them back to Him. This is also why Paul magnified his ministry to the Gentiles, hoping to save some of his countrymen by provoking them to jealousy.

> **Romans 11:11-15 (NIV)** **¹¹Again I ask: Did they stumble so as to fall beyond recovery? Not at all! Rather, because of their transgression, salvation has come to the Gentiles to make Israel envious. ¹²But if their transgression means riches for the world, and their loss means riches for the Gentiles, how much greater riches will their fullness bring! ¹³I am talking to you Gentiles. In as much as I am the apostle to the Gentiles, I make much of my ministry ¹⁴in the hope that**

I may somehow arouse my own people to envy and save some of them. ¹⁵For if their rejection is the reconciliation of the world, what will their acceptance be but life from the dead?

Paul then directs his attention to the Gentile believers, explaining that their obedience allowed them to be "grafted" into Israel to replace those removed by their own disobedience. This "grafting" however, is permanent only as long as they remain faithful. In addition, if any Israelites repent of their unbelief, they too can be grafted back in.

Romans 11:16-24 (NIV) ¹⁶If the part of the dough offered as firstfruits is holy, then the whole batch is holy; if the root is holy, so are the branches. ¹⁷If some of the branches have been broken off, and you, though a wild olive shoot, have been grafted in among the others and now share in the nourishing sap from the olive root, ¹⁸do not boast over those branches. If you do, consider this: You do not support the root, but the root supports you. ¹⁹You will say then, "Branches were broken off so that I could be grafted in." ²⁰Granted. But they were broken off because of unbelief, and you stand by faith. Do not be arrogant, but be afraid. ²¹For if God did not spare the natural branches, he will not spare you either. ²²Consider therefore the kindness and sternness of God: sternness to those who fell, but kindness to you, provided that you continue in his kindness. Otherwise, you also will be cut off. 23And if they do not persist in unbelief, they will be grafted in, for God is able to graft them in again. 24After all, if you were cut out of an olive tree that is wild by nature, and contrary to nature were grafted into a cultivated olive tree, how much more readily will these, the natural branches, be grafted into their own olive tree!

As Paul draws to a conclusion, he explains that this is how "all Israel" will be saved. Through a "hardening in part" mercy can now be shown to the Gentiles, and by showing mercy to the Gentiles, mercy will be available to disobedient Israel. In this way, Paul can say that, "God has committed them all to disobedience, that He might have mercy on all", proving that God is no respecter of persons and makes His plan of salvation available to all.

Romans 11:25-32 (NIV) 25I do not want you to be ignorant of this mystery, brothers, so that you may not be conceited: Israel has experienced a hardening in part until the full number of the Gentiles has come in. 26And so all Israel will be saved, as it is written: "The deliverer will come from Zion; he will turn godlessness away from Jacob. 27And this is my covenant with them when I take away their sins." 28As far as the gospel is concerned, they are enemies on your account; but as far as election is concerned, they are loved on account of the patriarchs, 29for God's gifts and his call are irrevocable. 30Just as you who were at one time disobedient to God have now received mercy as a result of their disobedience, 31so they too have now become disobedient in order that they too may now receive mercy as a result of God's mercy to you. 32For God has bound all men over to disobedience so that he may have mercy on them all.

Paul ends this section with a doxology, praising the wisdom and knowledge of God.

Romans 11:33-36 (NIV)   33Oh, the depth of the riches of the wisdom and knowledge of God! How unsearchable his judgments, and his paths beyond tracing out! 34"Who has known the mind of the Lord? Or who has been his counselor?" 35"Who has ever given to God, that God should repay him?" 36For from him and through him and to him are all things. To him be the glory forever! Amen.

REVIEW QUESTIONS FOR THE CHAPTER

1) List the main points of this chapter

_____

_____

2) What example does Paul use to show that God has not totally rejected the people of Israel? **(1)**

_____

_____

3) Why did God harden the rebellious Jews? **(11-12)**

_____

_____

4) Why was salvation allowed to come to the Gentiles? **(11-14)**

_____

_____

5) What condition is necessary to remain in the "tree of Israel?" **(20-23)**

_____

_____

6) How will "all Israel" be saved? (**25-26**)

_____

_____

7) What is Paul's summary on God's dealings with Israel? (**32**)

_____

_____

Chapter Twelve

OBJECTIVES IN STUDYING THIS CHAPTER

1) To see the difference between conformation and transformation, understanding the process involved in being transformed.
2) To appreciate the diversity of service in the Body of Christ.

OUTLINE

I. AN APPEAL TO CONSECRATION (1-2)

A. PRESENT YOUR BODIES AS LIVING SACRIFICES (1)
   1. In view of the mercies of God (**1a**)
   2. Which is your reasonable (spiritual, NAS) service (**1b**)

B. BE TRANSFORMED, NOT CONFORMED TO THE WORLD (2)
1. By the renewing of your mind (**2a**)
2. To prove the good, acceptable, and perfect will of God (**2b**)

II. SERVE GOD AS MEMBERS OF ONE BODY (3-8)

A. WITH HUMILITY (3)
1. In all seriousness (**3a**)
2. For what we are come form God (**3b**)

B. WITH APPRECIATION FOR DIVERSITY (4-5)
1. Members do not have the same function (**4**)
2. But we are one, members of one another (**5**)

C. WITH ZEAL, NO MATTER WHAT OUR GIFTS (6-8)

III. MISCELLANEOUS EXHORTATIONS (9-21)

A. AS CHRISTIANS (9-16)
1. Concerning love, good and evil (**9**)
2. Loving and honoring brethren (**10**)
3. Fervent in our service (**11**)
4. Rejoicing, patient, prayerful (**12**)
5. Caring for saints (**13**)
6. Blessing our enemies (**14**)
7. Sharing joys and sorrows (**15**)
8. Humble in our relations together (**16**)

B. RESPONDING TO EVIL (17-21)
1. Do not repay with evil, be mindful of what is good (**17**)
2. If possible, be at peace (**18**)
3. Give place to the wrath of God (**19**)
4. Overcome evil by responding with good (**20-21**)

SUMMARY

Having concluded his discourses concerning the gospel (**chapters 1-8**) and God's dealings with the nation of Israel (**chapters 9-11**), Paul now exhorts his readers to full service in the kingdom of God.

He begins with a plea to present their bodies as living sacrifices and to be transformed by the renewing of their minds, so that they can demonstrate in themselves that the will of God is good, acceptable, and perfect.

> *Romans 12:1-2 (NIV)* *¹Therefore, I urge you, brothers, in view of God's mercy, to offer your bodies as living sacrifices, holy and pleasing to God—this is your spiritual act of worship. ²Do not conform any longer to the pattern of this world, but be transformed by the renewing of your mind. Then you will be able to test and approve what God's will is— his good, pleasing and perfect will.*

He then encourages them to fulfill their proper place in the Body of Christ with proper humility and zeal.

> **Romans 12:3-8 (NIV)** **³For by the grace given me I say to every one of you: Do not think of yourself more highly than you ought, but rather think of yourself with sober judgment, in accordance with the measure of faith God has given you. ⁴Just as each of us has one body with many members, and these members do not all have the same function, ⁵so in Christ we who are many form one body, and each member belongs to all the others. ⁶We have different gifts, according to the grace given us. If a man's gift is prophesying, let him use it in proportion to his faith. ⁷If it is serving, let him serve; if it is teaching, let him teach; ⁸if it is encouraging, let him encourage; if it is contributing to the needs of others, let him give generously; if it is leadership, let him govern diligently; if it is showing mercy, let him do it cheerfully.**

Finally, there are a list of commands which are to govern the Christian's life and attitude towards love, good and evil, brethren in the Lord, service to God, and response to persecution.

> **Romans 12:9-21 (NIV)** **⁹Love must be sincere. Hate what is evil; cling to what is good. ¹⁰Be devoted to one another in**

brotherly love. Honor one another above yourselves. ¹¹Never be lacking in zeal, but keep your spiritual fervor, serving the Lord. ¹²Be joyful in hope, patient in affliction, faithful in prayer. ¹³Share with God's people who are in need. Practice hospitality. ¹⁴Bless those who persecute you; bless and do not curse. ¹⁵Rejoice with those who rejoice; mourn with those who mourn. ¹⁶Live in harmony with one another. Do not be proud, but be willing to associate with people of low position. Do not be conceited. ¹⁷Do not repay anyone evil for evil. Be careful to do what is right in the eyes of everybody. 18If it is possible, as far as it depends on you, live at peace with everyone. ¹⁹Do not take revenge, my friends, but leave room for God's wrath, for it is written: "It is mine to avenge; I will repay," says the Lord. ²⁰On the contrary: "If your enemy is hungry, feed him; if he is thirsty, give him something to drink. In doing this, you will heap burning coals on his head." ²¹Do not be overcome by evil, but overcome evil with good.

REVIEW QUESTIONS FOR THE CHAPTER

1) List the main points of this chapter

_____

_____

2) Upon what does Paul make his plea? **(1)**

_____

_____

3) How is a Christian to present himself before God? **(1)**

_____

_____

4) How is one transformed? **(2)**

_____

_____

5) What is the purpose of such transformation? **(2)**

_____

_____

6) What illustration shows our dependence upon each other in the church? (**4-5**)

_____

_____

7) How are Christians to respond to evil? (**19-21**)

_____

_____

Chapter Thirteen

OBJECTIVES IN STUDYING THIS CHAPTER

1) To understand our relationship to the government
2) To appreciate the importance of love and moral purity

OUTLINE

I. RESPONSIBILITIES TO THE GOVERNMENT (1-7)

A. BE IN SUBJECTION (1-5)
   1. For governing authorities are appointed by God (**1-2**)
   2. For governing authorities are God's ministers to avenge evil (**3-4**)

3. To avoid wrath and maintain good conscience (**5**)

B. FULFILL WHAT IS DUE (6-7)
1. Taxes, customs (**6-7a**)
2. Fear (respect), honor (**7b**)

II. <u>**EXHORTATION TO LOVE AND MORAL PURITY**</u> (8-14)

A. THE VALUE OF LOVE (8-10)
1. Owe no one anything but love (**8a**)
2. For love does no harm, and fulfills the Law (**8b-10**)

B. CONCERNING MORAL PURITY (11-14)
1. The time is short, we need to cast off the works of darkness and put on the armor of light (**11-12**)
2. Walk properly by putting on the Lord Jesus and making no provision to fulfill fleshly lusts (**13-14**)

SUMMARY

Continuing to instruct concerning the "transformed life," Paul now discusses the Christian's responsibilities to governmental authorities. Understanding that all governments are in power due to the providence of God, and that they serve as ministers of God to avenge the evil doer, Christians are admonished to submit to "the powers that be."

> *Romans 13:1-5 (NIV)* *¹Everyone must submit himself to the governing authorities, for there is no authority except that which God has established. The authorities that exist have been established by God. ²Consequently, he who rebels against the authority is rebelling against what God has instituted, and those who do so will bring judgment on themselves. ³For rulers hold no terror for those who do right, but for those who do wrong. Do you want to be free from fear of the one in authority? Then do what is right and he will commend you. ⁴For he is God's servant to do you good. But if you do wrong, be afraid, for he does not bear the sword for nothing. He is God's servant, an agent of wrath to bring punishment on the wrongdoer. ⁵Therefore, it is necessary to submit to the authorities, not only because of possible punishment but also because of conscience.*

This submission involves payment of taxes and having respect for those in authority.

> *Romans 13:6-7 (NIV)* *⁶This is also why you pay taxes, for the authorities are God's servants, who give their full time to governing. ⁷Give everyone what you owe him: If you owe taxes, pay taxes; if revenue, then revenue; if respect, then respect; if honor, then honor.*

Paul's next exhortation deals with the importance of love and moral purity. Christians are to be indebted to no one, save to love one another. When love is properly demonstrated, even the requirements of the Law are adequately met.

> **Romans 13:8-10 (NIV)** **⁸Let no debt remain outstanding, except the continuing debt to love one another, for he who loves his fellowman has fulfilled the law. ⁹The commandments, "Do not commit adultery," "Do not murder," "Do not steal," "Do not covet," and whatever other commandment there may be, are summed up in this one rule: "Love your neighbor as yourself." ¹⁰Love does no harm to its neighbor. Therefore love is the fulfillment of the law.**

This admonition to love, however, is carefully balanced with the reminder that time is short and it is imperative that Christians maintain moral purity. This is done by Christians putting on the Lord Jesus and not making provision for the fulfilling of the lusts of the flesh.

> **Romans 13:11-14 (NIV)** **¹¹And do this, understanding the present time. The hour has come for you to wake up from your slumber, because our salvation is nearer now than when we first believed. ¹²The night is nearly over; the day is almost here. So let us put aside the deeds of darkness and put on the armor of light. ¹³Let us behave decently, as in the daytime, not in orgies**

and drunkenness, not in sexual immorality and debauchery, not in dissension and jealousy. ¹⁴Rather, clothe yourselves with the Lord Jesus Christ, and do not think about how to gratify the desires of the sinful nature.

REVIEW QUESTIONS FOR THE CHAPTER

1) List the main points of the chapter

_____

_____

2) What one word summarizes the Christian's responsibility to the government? **(1)**

_____

_____

3) From where do governments get their authority? **(1)**

_____

_____

4) What happens if we resist governing authorities? **(2)**

_____

_____

5) What is a major responsibility of government? **(4)**

_____

_____

6) What should serve as motivation for Christian's submission to the government? **(5)**

_____

_____

7) What else is required of Christians in regard to government? **(7)**

_____

_____

8) What one thing should we owe to others? **(8)**

_____

_____

9) What are we to put on? **(12,14)**

_____

_____

10) What are we not to provide opportunities for? **(14)**

_____

_____

Chapter Fourteen

OBJECTIVES IN STUDYING THIS CHAPTER

1) To learn how strong and weak brethren should deal with one another
2) To see the importance of being true to our conscience

OUTLINE

I. <u>ADMONITIONS TO STRONG AND WEAK BRETHREN</u> (1-13)

A. HOW TO TREAT EACH OTHER (1-4)
1. The strong are to receive and not despise the weak (**1-3a**)
2. The weak are not to judge those God approves (**3b-4**)

B. HOW TO BE TRUE TO THE LORD IN THESE MATTERS (5-9)

1. Be fully convinced in your own mind (**5**)
2. Do what you do as to the Lord (**6-9**)

C. **DO NOT JUDGE ONE ANOTHER (10-13)**
1. Christ is to be our judge (**10-13a**)
2. Our concern should be not to put stumbling blocks in a brother's way (**13b**)

II. **FURTHER ADMONITIONS TO STRONG BRETHREN (14-23)**

A. **DO NOT DESTROY A BROTHER FOR WHOM CHRIST DIED (14-18)**
1. Food is harmless in itself, but we can misuse it to the destruction of those who are weak (**14-16**)
2. The kingdom of God is more important than food and drink (**17-18**)

B. **PURSUE THINGS WHICH MAKE FOR PEACE (19-23)**
1. Build up your brother, don't destroy him over food (**19-20**)
2. Be willing to forego your liberties for the sake of your brother (**21**)
3. Appreciate the importance of a clear conscience in your weak brother (**22-23**)

SUMMARY

In this chapter Paul discusses the relationship strong and weak brethren are to have toward each other. He admonishes the strong to be careful in their dealings with those whose faith and knowledge is weak, and for the weak not to judge those who are doing what God allows.

> **Romans 14:1-4 (NIV)** **¹Accept him whose faith is weak, without passing judgment on disputable matters. ²One man's faith allows him to eat everything, but another man, whose faith is weak, eats only vegetables. ³The man who eats everything must not look down on him who does not, and the man who does not eat everything must not condemn the man who does, for God has accepted him. ⁴Who are you to judge someone else's servant? To his own master he stands or falls. And he will stand, for the Lord is able to make him stand.**

In such matters, each brother should be true to their conscience and do what they do as service rendered to the Lord.

> **Romans 14:5-9 (NIV)** **⁵One man considers one day more sacred than another; another man considers every day alike. Each one should be fully convinced in his own mind. ⁶He who regards one day as special, does so to the Lord. He who eats meat, eats to the Lord, for he gives thanks to God; and he**

who abstains, does so to the Lord and gives thanks to God. ⁷For none of us lives to himself alone and none of us dies to himself alone. ⁸If we live, we live to the Lord; and if we die, we die to the Lord. So, whether we live or die, we belong to the Lord. ⁹For this very reason, Christ died and returned to life so that he might be the Lord of both the dead and the living.

There is no place for condemning or despising one another in these matters, for Jesus will be the judge.

Romans 14:10-12 (NIV) ¹⁰You, then, why do you judge your brother? Or why do you look down on your brother? For we will all stand before God's judgment seat. ¹¹It is written: " 'As surely as I live,' says the Lord, 'every knee will bow before me; every tongue will confess to God.' " ¹²So then, each of us will give an account of himself to God.

Of primary concern is not to put stumbling blocks in a brother's way.

Romans 14:13 (NIV) Therefore let us stop passing judgment on one another. Instead, make up your mind not to put any stumbling block or obstacle in your brother's way.

The importance of being true to one's own conscience, and not encouraging the weak brother to violate his own, is the emphasis of the last half of the chapter. Things harmless within themselves can destroy those whose consciences do not permit them, so those who understand the true nature of the kingdom of God will be willing to forego personal liberties to maintain peace and build up their weaker brethren.

> *Romans 14:14-23 (NIV)* ¹⁴*As one who is in the Lord Jesus, I am fully convinced that no food is unclean in itself. But if anyone regards something as unclean, then for him it is unclean.* ¹⁵*If your brother is distressed because of what you eat, you are no longer acting in love. Do not by your eating destroy your brother for whom Christ died.* ¹⁶*Do not allow what you consider good to be spoken of as evil.* ¹⁷*For the kingdom of God is not a matter of eating and drinking, but of righteousness, peace and joy in the Holy Spirit,* ¹⁸*because anyone who serves Christ in this way is pleasing to God and approved by men.* ¹⁹*Let us therefore make every effort to do what leads to peace and to mutual edification.* ²⁰*Do not destroy the work of God for the sake of food. All food is clean, but it is wrong for a man to eat anything that causes someone else to stumble.* ²¹*It is better not to eat meat or drink wine or to do anything else that will cause your brother to fall.* ²²*So whatever you believe about these things keep between yourself and God. Blessed is the man who does not condemn himself by what he approves.* ²³*But the man who has*

doubts is condemned if he eats, because his eating is not from faith; and everything that does not come from faith is sin.

REVIEW QUESTIONS FOR THE CHAPTER

1) List the main points of this chapter

_____

_____

2) How are strong and weak brethren to treat each other? (**3**)

_____

_____

3) What is important according to verse 5?

_____

_____

4) In all matters, whom is it we should try to please? (**6-8**)

_____

_____

5) Who will be the Judge in such matters? (**10-12**)

_____

_____

6) What is important according to verse 13?

_____

_____

7) What elements are crucial to the Kingdom of God? (**17**)

_____

_____

8) How far should one be willing to go to avoid causing a brother to stumble? (**21**)

_____

_____

9) If we violate our conscience, what are we guilty of? (**23**)

_____

_____

Chapter Fifteen

OBJECTIVES IN STUDYING THIS CHAPTER

1) To see further the importance of being considerate of weak brethren
2) To be impressed with the example of the churches in Macedonia and Achaia in their liberality toward the church in Jerusalem.

OUTLINE

I. <u>CONCLUDING ADMONITIONS TO STRONG BRETHREN</u> (1-13)

A. BEAR WITH THE SCRUPLES OF THE WEAK (1-6)
1. Try to please your brethren, as Christ did (**1-3**)

2. With the help of God and Scripture, be patient, so you may with one mind and mouth glorify God (**4-6**)

B. RECEIVE ONE ANOTHER (7-12)
1. As Christ received us, to the glory of God (**7**)
2. As Christ served Jews and Gentiles, in fulfillment of prophecy (**8-12**)

C. PAUL'S PRAYER FOR THEM (13)
1. That God might fill them with all joy and peace in believing (**13a**)
2. That they might abound in hope by the power of the Holy Spirit (**13b**)

II. PAUL'S PLANS TO SEE THEM (14-33)

A. THE REASON FOR WRITING THEM (14-21)
1. He is well aware of their own abilities (**14**)
2. Simply reminding them, as is appropriate from one who is a "minister to the Gentiles" (**15-16**)
3. Though he normally aims to preach where Christ has not been named (**17-21**)

B. HIS TRAVEL PLANS (22-29)
1. To go to Spain via Rome (**22-24**)
2. But first, to Jerusalem with a contribution form those in Macedonia and Achaia (**25-29**)

C. REQUEST FOR PRAYER, AND PRAYER FOR THEM (30-33)
1. His request for their prayers for his safe journeys (**30-32**)
2. His prayer that God be with them (**33**)

SUMMARY

Paul continues his discussion on how those who are strong are to receive and bear with the infirmities of the weak. Encouraging the strong to be concerned with uplifting the weak, he reminds them of Christ and His unselfishness.

> *Romans 15:1-3 (NIV)* ¹*We who are strong ought to bear with the failings of the weak and not to please ourselves. ²Each of us should please his neighbor for his good, to build him up. ³For even Christ did not please himself but, as it is written: "The insults of those who insult you have fallen on me."*

Reminding them of the value of the Old Testament Scriptures, he pleads for patience so that with one mind and one mouth they may glorify God.

> *Romans 15:4-6 (NIV)* ⁴*For everything that was written in the past was written to teach us, so that through endurance and the encouragement of the Scriptures we might have hope. ⁵May the God who gives endurance and encouragement give you a*

spirit of unity among yourselves as you follow Christ Jesus, ⁶so that with one heart and mouth you may glorify the God and Father of our Lord Jesus Christ.

Finally, he calls for them to receive one another to the glory of God, just as Christ served both Jews and Gentiles in fulfilling the prophets of old.

Romans 15:7-12 (NIV) ⁷Accept one another, then, just as Christ accepted you, in order to bring praise to God. ⁸For I tell you that Christ has become a servant of the Jews on behalf of God's truth, to confirm the promises made to the patriarchs ⁹so that the Gentiles may glorify God for his mercy, as it is written: "Therefore I will praise you among the Gentiles; I will sing hymns to your name." ¹⁰Again, it says, "Rejoice, O Gentiles, with his people." ¹¹And again, "Praise the Lord, all you Gentiles, and sing praises to him, all you peoples." ¹²And again, Isaiah says, "The Root of Jesse will spring up, one who will arise to rule over the nations; the Gentiles will hope in him."

Paul then offers a prayer that God might fill them with joy and peace in believing, so that they may abound in hope with the help of the Holy Spirit.

Romans 15:13 (NIV) May the God of hope fill you with all joy and peace as you trust in him, so that you may overflow with hope by the power of the Holy Spirit.

At this point, Paul begins to draw this epistle to a close by making remarks concerning his apostleship and plans to see them. Recognizing their own abilities in the faith, he still felt it appropriate to write to them as he did.

> **Romans 15:14-16 (NIV)** **¹⁴I myself am convinced, my brothers, that you yourselves are full of goodness, complete in knowledge and competent to instruct one another. ¹⁵I have written you quite boldly on some points, as if to remind you of them again, because of the grace God gave me ¹⁶to be a minister of Christ Jesus to the Gentiles with the priestly duty of proclaiming the gospel of God, so that the Gentiles might become an offering acceptable to God, sanctified by the Holy Spirit.**

Speaking of his design not to preach where Christ had already been received.

> **Romans 15:17-21 (NIV) ¹⁷Therefore I glory in Christ Jesus in my service to God. ¹⁸I will not venture to speak of anything except what Christ has accomplished through me in leading the Gentiles to obey God by what I have said and done— ¹⁹by the power of signs and miracles, through the power of the Spirit. So from Jerusalem all the way around to Illyricum, I have fully proclaimed the gospel of Christ. ²⁰It has always been my ambition to preach the gospel where Christ**

> *was not known, so that I would not be building on someone else's foundation. 21Rather, as it is written: "Those who were not told about him will see, and those who have not heard will understand."*

Paul tells of his plan to come to Rome on his way to Spain.

> ***Romans 15:22-24 (NIV)** 22This is why I have often been hindered from coming to you. 23But now that there is no more place for me to work in these regions, and since I have been longing for many years to see you, 24I plan to do so when I go to Spain. I hope to visit you while passing through and to have you assist me on my journey there, after I have enjoyed your company for a while.*

But first, he is going to the poor saints in Jerusalem with a contribution from the saints in Macedonia and Achaia.

> ***Romans 15:25-29 (NIV)** 25Now, however, I am on my way to Jerusalem in the service of the saints there. 26For Macedonia and Achaia were pleased to make a contribution for the poor among the saints in Jerusalem. 27They were pleased to do it, and indeed they owe it to them. For if the Gentiles have shared in the Jews' spiritual blessings, they owe it to the Jews to share with them their material blessings. 28So after I have completed this task and have made*

sure that they have received this fruit, I will go to Spain and visit you on the way. ²⁹I know that when I come to you, I will come in the full measure of the blessing of Christ.

Realizing the danger such a trip entails, he asks to be remembered in their prayers.

Romans 15:30-33 (NIV) ³⁰I urge you, brothers, by our Lord Jesus Christ and by the love of the Spirit, to join me in my struggle by praying to God for me. ³¹Pray that I may be rescued from the unbelievers in Judea and that my service in Jerusalem may be acceptable to the saints there, ³²so that by God's will I may come to you with joy and together with you be refreshed. ³³The God of peace be with you all. Amen.

REVIEW QUESTIONS FOR THE CHAPTER

1) List the main points of this chapter

_____

_____

2) Whose example are we to follow in bearing the weakness of others? (**1-3**)

_____

_____

3) What value is the Old Testament to Christians? (**4**)

_____

_____

4) Why is it important that we be of one mind? (**5-6**)

_____

_____

5) To what degree are we to receive one another? (**7**)

_____

_____

6) In his preaching, what did Paul try to avoid? (**20**)

_____

_____

7) Where did Paul hope to go after passing through Rome? (**24**)

_____

_____

8) Where was he headed for at the time he wrote this epistle? Why? (**25**)

_____

_____

Chapter Sixteen

OBJECTIVES IN STUDYING THIS CHAPTER

1) To be impressed with such Christians as Phoebe, Priscilla, and Aquila
2) To understand the warning against those who cause division.

OUTLINE

I. CONCLUDING INSTRUCTIONS & FAREWELLS (1-24)

A. COMMENDATION OF PHOEBE (1-2)
   1. A servant of the church in Cenchrea (**1**)
   2. To receive her in a worthy manner, helping her along (**2**)

B. MISCELLANEOUS GREETINGS FROM PAUL (3-16)
1. To Priscilla and Aquila (**3-5a**)
2. To various others (**5b-16**)

C. A FINAL WARNING (17-20)
1. Against those who selfishly cause divisions and offenses (**17-18**)
2. To continue in obedience, for God will give them victory (**19-20**)

D. GREETINGS FROM PAUL'S COMPANIONS (21-24)
1. From Timothy and others (**21**)
2. From Tertius, Paul's "amanuensis" [personal scribe] (**22**)
3. From brethren at Corinth (**23-24**)

II. <u>PAUL'S DOXOLOGY</u> (25-27)

A. TO HIM WHO IS ABLE TO ESTABLISH YOU (25-26)
1. According to the gospel and preaching of Jesus Christ (**25a**)
2. According to the mystery once secret, but now revealed and made known to all nations (**25b-26**)
3. Made known by the prophetic Scriptures (**26a**)
4. Made known for obedience to the faith (**26b**)

III. TO GOD, ALONE WISE, BE GLORY THROUGH JESUS CHRIST FOREVER (27)

SUMMARY

In this last chapter, Paul closes with miscellaneous instructions, greetings, warnings, and a doxology. Of particular note are his comments concerning Phoebe, a servant of the church in Cenchrea.

> ***Romans 16:1-2 (NIV)** [1] **I commend to you our sister Phoebe, a servant of the church in Cenchrea.** [2] **I ask you to receive her in the Lord in a way worthy of the saints and to give her any help she may need from you, for she has been a great help to many people, including me.***

Also, his greetings to Priscilla and Aquila remind us of how instrumental this couple was in the spread of the gospel.

> ***Romans 16:3-5a (NIV)** [3] **Greet Priscilla and Aquila, my fellow workers in Christ Jesus.** [4] **They risked their lives for me. Not only I but all the churches of the Gentiles are grateful to them.** [5(a)] **Greet also the church that meets at their house...***

The remaining greetings from Paul remind us that there were many others who contributed to the growth of the church in the first century.

> ***Romans 16:5b-16 (NIV)** [5(b)] **Greet my dear friend Epenetus, who was the first convert to Christ in the province of Asia.** [6] **Greet Mary, who worked very hard for you.** [7] **Greet***

Andronicus and Junias, my relatives who have been in prison with me. They are outstanding among the apostles, and they were in Christ before I was. ⁸Greet Ampliatus, whom I love in the Lord. ⁹Greet Urbanus, our fellow worker in Christ, and my dear friend Stachys. ¹⁰Greet Apelles, tested and approved in Christ. Greet those who belong to the household of Aristobulus. ¹¹Greet Herodion, my relative. Greet those in the household of Narcissus who are in the Lord. ¹²Greet Tryphena and Tryphosa, those women who work hard in the Lord. Greet my dear friend Persis, another woman who has worked very hard in the Lord. ¹³Greet Rufus, chosen in the Lord, and his mother, who has been a mother to me, too. ¹⁴Greet Asyncritus, Phlegon, Hermes, Patrobas, Hermas and the brothers with them. ¹⁵Greet Philologus, Julia, Nereus and his sister, and Olympas and all the saints with them. ¹⁶Greet one another with a holy kiss. All the churches of Christ send greetings.

A final warning is given against those who would cause divisions and occasions of stumbling contrary to what Paul had taught in this epistle.

Romans 16:17-18 (NIV)   ¹⁷I urge you, brothers, to watch out for those who cause divisions and put obstacles in your way that are contrary to the teaching you have learned. Keep away from them. ¹⁸For such people are not serving our Lord Christ, but

> *their own appetites. By smooth talk and flattery they deceive the minds of naive people.*

For above all else, Paul wanted to ensure their continued obedience in the gospel.

> *Romans 16:19-20 (NIV) [19]Everyone has heard about your obedience, so I am full of joy over you; but I want you to be wise about what is good, and innocent about what is evil. [20]The God of peace will soon crush Satan under your feet. The grace of our Lord Jesus be with you.*

Paul's companions at Corinth add their greetings.

> *Romans 16:21-24 (NIV) [21]Timothy, my fellow worker, sends his greetings to you, as do Lucius, Jason and Sosipater, my relatives. [22]I, Tertius, who wrote down this letter, greet you in the Lord. [23]Gaius, whose hospitality I and the whole church here enjoy, sends you his greetings. Erastus, who is the city's director of public works, and our brother Quartus send you their greetings.*

And Paul closes this wonderful epistle with an expression of praise to God for the revelation of the gospel which was leading to the obedience of faith among all nations.

Romans 16:25-27 (NIV) *²⁵Now to him who is able to establish you by my gospel and the proclamation of Jesus Christ, according to the revelation of the mystery hidden for long ages past, ²⁶but now revealed and made known through the prophetic writings by the command of the eternal God, so that all nations might believe and obey him— ²⁷to the only wise God be glory forever through Jesus Christ! Amen.*

REVIEW QUESTIONS FOR THIS CHAPTER

1) List the main points of this chapter

_____

_____

2) How does Paul describe Phoebe? (**1-2**)

_____

_____

3) How does Paul describe Priscilla and Aquila? (**3-4**)

_____

_____

4) How does Paul describe those who cause division and offenses? (**18**)

_____

_____

5) Is the "mystery" referred to in verse 25 still hidden? (**25-26**)

_____

_____

6) What is the objective of the gospel according to verse 26?

_____
_____

ANSWERS TO END OF CHAPTER QUESTIONS:

Introduction:

1) The apostle Paul (1:1)

2) Corinth

3) 57 or 58 A.D.

4) To set straight the design and nature of the gospel

5) Romans 1:16-17

Chapter One:

1) -Introduction (1-17)
   -The Gentiles' Need of Salvation (18-32)

2) With power, through His resurrection from the dead

3) To bring about the obedience of faith among all nations

4) To see them and share in their faith together

5) Both to Greeks and barbarians, both to wise and unwise

6) The gospel of Christ

7) In it the righteousness of God is revealed

8) His eternal power and Godhead (divine nature)

9) By "giving people up" to their own sinful passions

10) Homosexuality

Chapter Two:

1) -The Gentiles' Need of Salvation (1-16)
   -The Jew's Need of Salvation (17-29)

2) They are guilty of the same thing and so condemn themselves

3) Through kindness, forbearance, and longsuffering

4) Eternal life to those who do good; wrath and indignation, tribulation and anguish to those who do evil.

5) The law of their conscience will condemn them when God judges the secrets of their hearts by Jesus Christ

6) "By nature" (note the definition above); they are able to do the things contained in the Law, for they have the "work of the Law" written in their hearts.

7) Through inconsistency and disobedience to the Law, they dishonored God.

Chapter Three:

1) -The Jews' Need of Salvation (1-20)
   -The Provision: Justification By Faith (21-31)

2) They possessed the revealed oracles of God

3) The knowledge of sin

4) The righteousness of God (God's way of justifying sinful man)

5) All have sinned

6) Being justified through the redemption that is in Christ Jesus

7) Through the blood of Jesus Christ

8) By faith

9) It does not void the need for law, but rather supports the demand of law

Chapter Four:

1) Justification of Abraham as an example (1-8)

2) By believing in God to justify the ungodly (and not in his own works)

3) In the sense that man's sins are not counted against him.

4) By his being justified by faith prior to his circumcision

5) The righteousness of faith

6) By fathering Isaac

7) Those who believe that God raised Jesus from the dead

Chapter Five:

1) The Blessings of Justification (1-11)
   Comparing Christ with Adam (12-21)

2) Peace with God, access to grace, rejoicing in hope

3) Knowing trials can produce perseverance, character and hope

4) By having Christ die for us when we were still sinners

5) His present life, which saves us from the wrath to come

6) Death - Paul means physical death

7) Just as Adam through his sin brought physical death to all, so Christ through His obedience will give life to all (through the resurrection – cf. 1 Corinthians 15:21-22)
But Christ does even more; to those who will receive it, he offers "an abundance of grace and the gift of righteousness" so they can reign in life through Jesus (cf. v. 17)

8) Grace

Chapter Six:

1) -We Are Dead to Sin! (1-14)
-We Should Be Slaves To God! (15-23)

2) Because we died to sin

3) They are baptized into His death, being buried with Him and united with Him in the likeness of His death, where the old man is crucified with Him and the body of sin is done away, making it possible to be freed from sin and to rise to walk in newness of life

4) As instruments of righteousness to God

5) Because the Christian is not "under law" but "under grace"

6) To obey the doctrine of God from the heart

7) Holiness, or sanctification

8) Being set free from sin; becoming slaves to God; bearing the fruit of holiness

9) Death; eternal life

Chapter Seven:

1) -Jewish Believers and the Law (1-6)
   -Limitations of the Law (7-25)

2) Those who know the law (Jewish Christians)

3) How a woman whose husband dies is free to be married to another without being guilty of adultery

4) Dead to the law, delivered from the law

5) To illustrate his point, Paul mentions "you shall not covet," one of the Ten Commandments

6) No! It was "sin" that produced death

7) The DESIRE to do good and avoid evil may be there, but the ABILITY is found lacking

8) CAPTIVITY to the law (or principle) of sin in one's members

9) From God, through Jesus Christ our Lord!

Chapter Eight:

1) -In Christ There is Freedom From Sin (1-17)
   -Blessings of Being Children of God (18-39)

2) The Law of Moses could not set one free from the "law of sin and death"

3) Death; life and peace

4) Yes

5) By putting to death the deeds of the body with the help of the Spirit

6) -One day we will be glorified together with Christ
   -We have the help of the Holy Spirit
   -All things ultimately work for our good
   -Nothing can separate us from God's love

Chapter Nine:

1) -Paul's Concern for His Brethren of Israel (1-5)
   -The True Children of God (6-29)

-The Basis of God's Choice: Faith vs. No Faith

2) Enough to be lost if it would do any good

3) Children of promise, not children of flesh

4) To show mercy on who He wills, and to harden who He wills

5) Hosea

6) Only a remnant would be saved

7) Because of faith

8) They trusted more in the keeping of the Law, and did not believe in Christ

Chapter Ten:

1) -Israel's Refusal of God's Righteousness (1-15)
   -Israel's Neglect of the Gospel (16-21)

2) That they may be saved

3) -They have a zeal for God
   -But not according to knowledge

4) In ignorance they were seeking to establish their own righteousness

5) -The Lord Jesus (or, that Jesus is Lord)
   -That God raised Jesus from the dead

6) Whoever believes and calls upon the name of the Lord

7) The sending out of preachers

8) By hearing the word of God

9) Yes, for the gospel had been spread to the ends of the world

10) By making Himself manifest to those who had not been seeking Him (the Gentiles)

Chapter Eleven:

1) -God Has Not Totally Rejected Israel (1-10)
   -Hardening Of Israel to Benefit Israel (11-32)
   -Paul's Hymn Of Praise to God (33-36)

2) Himself

3) So salvation might be presented to the Gentiles

4) To provoke the rebellious Jews to jealousy that they might repent

5) Continuing in faith

6) By a partial hardening of Israel, to allow Gentiles to come in and to provoke rebellious Jews to repent

7) "God has committed them all to disobedience, that He might have mercy on all"

Chapter Twelve:

1) -An Appeal to Consecration (1-2)
   -Serve God As Members of One Body (3-8)
   -Miscellaneous Exhortations (9-21)

2) The mercies of God; their reasonable service

3) As a living sacrifice, holy, acceptable of God

4) By the renewing of their minds

5) To prove (demonstrate) what is the good, acceptable, and perfect will of God

6) Members of a body

7) In a positive way, with good

Chapter Thirteen:

1) -Responsibilities To the Government (1-7)
   -Exhortations to Love and Moral Purity (8-14)

2) Submit

3) God

4) We resist God and bring judgment upon ourselves

5) To avenge the evil doer

6) Wrath, and conscience

7) Payment of taxes, and respect for those in authority

8) Love

9) The "armor of light", the Lord Jesus Christ

10) The fulfillment of fleshly lusts

Chapter Fourteen:

1) -Admonitions To Strong and Weak Brethren (1-13)
   -Further Admonitions To Strong Brethren (14-23)

2) -The strong are not to despise the weak
   -The weak are not to judge the strong

3) "Let each be fully convinced in his own mind"

4) The Lord

5) The Lord

6) Not to put a stumbling block or a cause to fall in our brother's way

7) Righteousness, peace, and joy in the Holy Spirit

8) As far as giving up personal liberties in Christ

9) Sin

Chapter Fifteen:

1) -Concluding Admonitions to Strong Brethren (1-13)
   -Paul's Plans to See Them (14-33)

2) Christ's

3) To learn, to find patience and comfort, to increase hope

4) So we may in unity of mind and mouth glorify God

5) As Christ received us; to the glory of God

6) Preaching where Christ had already been preached

7) Spain

8) Jerusalem; to minister the contribution form Macedonia and Achaia for the poor saints in Jerusalem

Chapter Sixteen:

1) -Concluding Instructions and Farewells (1-24)
   -Paul's Doxology (25-27)

2) A servant of the church; a helper of Paul and of many

3) Fellow workers; who risked their necks for Paul's life

4) They serve not the Lord, but their own belly

5) No, it has been revealed and made known through preaching and the Scriptures to all nations

6) Obedience to the Faith

Also by Dr. Christopher Bowen:

⇒ Some Assembly Required: 53 Illustrated Sermons for use as a Pastoral Help

⇒ That's My Story & I'm Sticking To It: A Personal Journey to Successful Ministry

⇒ Moving From Test, To Trial, To Triumph: The Journey of Job

⇒ Your Choice Life or Death! A Study of the Book of Revelation

If you would like to order more copies of this book or any of the other books available by Dr. Bowen.

Dr. Christopher Bowen
Living Faith International Ministries
5880 Old Dixie Road
Forest Park, Georgia 30297
(404) 361-0812

www.livingfaithtabernacle.com

DrCBowen@aol.com

www.ingramcontent.com/pod-product-compliance
Lightning Source LLC
LaVergne TN
LVHW011421080426
835512LV00005B/187